HITLER

HITLER

THE MAN AND THE MONSTER

MICHAEL KERRIGAN

amber
BOOKS

ISBN: 978-1-78274-504-4

Published by
Amber Books Ltd
74–77 White Lion Street
London
N1 9PF
United Kingdom
www.amberbooks.co.uk
Appstore: itunes.com/apps/amberbooksltd
Facebook: www.facebook.com/amberbooks
Twitter: @amberbooks

Project editor: Michael Spilling
Design: Jerry Williams
Picture research: Terry Forshaw

Manufactured in China

1 4 6 8 10 9 7 5 3 2

CONTENTS

INTRODUCTION

How do we get the measure of a man who's more customarily seen as a monster?
How do we make sense of a personality who's become a demonic myth?
The vastness of his crimes only make it the more vital that we engage with
Hitler as the man he really was.

To understand all is to forgive all, says the proverb. But how much understanding would it take to make sense of a shattered continent, a poisoned morality, and more than 50 million lives? There's no doubt that Adolf Hitler stands out among the monstrous figures of modern history; not just for the scale of his crimes, but for the methodical way he went about them.

Cold War historians tried hard to make the case for Joseph Stalin as his match – or even his outdoer – in mass murder, but these arguments have not survived the subsequent

opening up of the Soviet state archives. Besides the 30 million of Stalin's countrymen killed by the invading Nazis, the communist dictator's 'Great Terror' scarcely seems to merit the description – although it was obviously bad enough for its one million or so victims. It would have been no consolation to the five million or so shot or starved in the course of the collectivization of Ukraine that they were dying in the name of ideological fanaticism rather than racism. For the most part, though, Stalin's mad paranoia – like that of China's Chairman Mao a couple of decades later – seems relatively rational beside Hitler's highly philosophized analysis of (and 'Final Solution' to) the so-called 'Jewish Problem'. Or, for that matter, the carefully articulated absurdities of his attitude towards

other targeted groups like the Roma, Poles and Slovenes, homosexuals, disabled people and Jehovah's Witnesses.

Even so, there is no doubt that Stalin knew a thing or two about atrocity. 'A single death is a tragedy; a million deaths is a statistic,' he reputedly said. A corollary of this rule would seem to be that the sheer enormity of the charge sheet against Adolf Hitler has made it all but impossible to know how to come to any kind of comprehension, first of Hitler, and then of his crimes themselves. We can visualize him, certainly: that almost crazy-comic toothbrush moustache and side-swept hair; we see him grimace and gesticulate as he delivers a ranting speech. We know a great deal *about* him – so much that the challenge for his biographer is less about locating than selecting material. But

Now, it seems, Hitler is an emblem; a reference point for those seeking to discredit enemies from Saddam Hussein and the Taliban to Barack Obama and Donald Trump. His association smears such otherwise blameless things as vegetarianism, interest in folklore, or enthusiasm for fresh air and hiking.

It would appear Hitler was both the witness and victim of domestic violence

LIFE AND WORKS

Where does all this leave Hitler's life? We invariably read a biography in hopes of its explaining or accounting for its subject's fame (or infamy). We can't help seeking some sort of equivalence – in background, education or experience – to the individual and what he or she achieved. With Hitler, though, there is a difficulty in coming up with what the poet and critic T.S. Eliot (1888–1965) called an 'objective correlative': some sort of equivalence between cause and consequence, which we are unlikely to find, can drive us into a hopeless spiral of speculation.

In embarking on any biography, especially one as comparatively brief as this, it has to be borne in mind that we can only sketch out possibilities, not establish explanations. We can state facts

in what sense can it be said that we know *him*?

ICON OF EVIL

It hardly helps that the Nazi leader has become the go-to comparison in all discussion of political tyranny and criminal atrocity; a sort of 'gold standard' in oppression and an absolute in evil. The further removed we are historically from Hitler and his world, the greater

his importance seems to grow. Mike Godwin's notorious (and only semi-humorous) 'law', that 'as an online discussion grows longer, the probability of a comparison involving Nazism or Hitler approaches 1' only underlines the way in which the reputation of the German dictator has transcended not just his personality but his place in what we have conventionally understood as 'history'.

where they are known (and there are many missing in Hitler's life story), but that is not the same as setting out the truth in all the comprehensiveness that requires.

As we'll see in Chapter 1, Hitler was the product of a dysfunctional family, where he would appear both to have been a witness and a victim of domestic violence. That family was itself a product of what was arguably a dysfunctional state in a time of social confusion and cultural crisis. So too were a great many others, however, and

Hitler promoted a powerful aesthetic of aggression and Germanic masculinity. Here, he salutes his Brownshirts at a Nuremberg show of strength in 1927.

although it is true that as *Führer* he was destined to find eager accomplices for his crimes, there was only ever going to be one Adolf Hitler. It's hard to see how these challenges in life could have created such monstrosity on such a scale.

MAN AND MYTH

It doesn't help that Hitler was himself so industrious a self-mythologizer, starting with his ranting memoir *Mein Kampf* ('My Struggle', 1925–6). But his biographers too have frequently succumbed to the temptation to take this larger-than-life character on his own vainglorious terms. This is true not just of the Nazi sympathizers of his own time or the apologists over the decades since; for his critics, too, his vast crimes have seemed to call for hyperbolic characterizations.

Some assessments have also assumed a retributive character, showing the need to degrade and (posthumously) humiliate. Hence reports of Hitler's homosexuality; his various sexual dysfunctions; his alleged 'micropenis'; his masochism; his coprophilia.... Ingenious arguments have been made to justify these claims, and all manner of 'evidence' mustered. In the end, we cannot categorically rule any of them out.

Right: A Father-figure for the Fatherland, Hitler meets young children: the guarantee of a glorious German future.

Opposite: A failed artist and yet still – quite literally – a visionary, Hitler launched not just an ideology but a 'look', as this poster shows.

We should recognize, however, that any persuasiveness they have as explanations of Hitler's character depends in large part on their appeal to emotion. Wouldn't it be perfect if the architect of the Final Solution turned out to have Jewish roots? If the Holocaust

had been ultimately motivated by self-hatred? Could Hitler's persecution of homosexuals have been driven by his own guilty desires, his long-running affair with Eva Braun some desperate attempt at overcompensation? Could his seeming determination to bring a

continent crashing around him have resulted from frustrated creativity, from his failure to achieve his first ambitions in the world of art?

LIFE vs TIMES

How far was Hitler's dictatorship actually dictated by the time he lived in? Did he delude himself that he was dominating his age and shaping its events? Is there a risk of our indulging his own heroic characterization of himself when his actual role was more passive? As we'll see, the Third Reich emerged in a time of traumatic change for Germany; the economic and cultural forces brought to bear on all of Europe were profound. Although by no means an intellectual giant, Hitler was an intellectual in the sense that he took ideas seriously, registered many of the main shifts in the scientific and philosophical thinking of his own time and sought, however clumsily, to find his own response. Chapter

2 attempts to show how much of Hitler's own developing philosophy, in all its crassness, might yet be seen to shadow the higher-flown thinking of his age.

It would be an exaggeration to see the young Hitler as a real contributor to the intense artistic and intellectual ferment of early-

This picture is a copy of a painting reputed to be by Hitler. Though severely limited, his artistic gifts were real.

Hitler relaxes in a Bavarian holiday home, about 1934. Nazism claimed to be deeply rooted in the beauties of the German landscape.

twentieth-century Vienna, as some kind of equal participant with Wittgenstein, Klimt and Freud. He would arguably end up being that grim golden age's logical conclusion, though, the dark and sinister secret at which its most glorious expressions always hinted. 'When you have gazed long into the abyss,' the philosopher Friedrich Nietzsche had observed, 'the abyss gazes back into you.' If Hitler's rise and reign were not abysmal, it's hard to imagine what might be.

To that extent, then, as horrific as it was, Hitler's Reich may be seen as having been 'appropriate' to its age. This brings us to another question: If Hitler had not existed, would he have had to be invented? The question is hard to answer,

and it is a relief that it doesn't need to be. He *did* exist, however we attempt to explain his formation or account for his rise to power. And he succeeded in constructing a state and society around himself.

Hitler could also be seen as having been a product of his times to the extent that he had unprecedented and unparalleled opportunity. No previous tyrant – Peisistratos, Genghis Khan, Tamerlane – could have called upon a state apparatus, an industrial infrastructure or a military capability of atrocities of this sophistication or scale. Even so, we are left with a perplexing riddle wrapped in an unsettling enigma. Try as we might to account for Hitler, he remains unique.

CHAPTER 1

CHILDHOOD

To suggest that Hitler's origins and early life were 'mysterious' would be unnecessarily melodramatic: but they were undoubtedly obscure; and important details remain unclear. Most elusive of all, however, is any sense – despite real and evident hardships and humiliations – of convincing explanations for the evil he'd eventually unleash.

Hitler's history was being assiduously rewritten even before it had properly begun. The process seems to have started with his father. In 1876, when he was pushing 40, although still without a son, Alois Schicklgruber took formal steps to change his name. A customs inspector in the little town of Braunau am Inn, in Upper Austria, he was from this time on known as Alois Hitler. He also had a 'legitimate' birth bestowed upon him retrospectively by a parish priest; hitherto he had been down as 'paternity unknown'.

Opposite: The class of 1899 – Adolf Hitler at primary school in Leonding, Austria. Hitler stands tall in the backrow, centre. He did not do particularly well in school, and left formal education in 1905.

DOUBTFUL PARENTAGE

Alois did not pluck his now-notorious surname out of nowhere. One Johann Georg Hiedler (1792–1857) had played a major part in his upbringing, having married Alois's mother, Maria Anna Schicklgruber, in 1842. Even so, it is not certain that this Johann Georg had been the boy's biological father: by the time they wed, Alois was five years old. Nor is that missing half-decade the only period of Maria Anna's life left unaccounted for: much remains mysterious about the months – even the years – before her baby's birth.

Forty-two years old and a domestic servant in the village of Döllerheim, in Lower Austria, Maria Anna Schicklgruber was not obviously a 'person of interest' from a historical point of view. Poor and uneducated, a menial toiler and a resident hanger-on in other people's households, she had no appreciable social status of her own. If she is a subject of scholarly investigation now, it is because of a grandson she never saw, and who wasn't born till more than 40 years after she had died.

Maria Anna was born in Strones, a little village in Waldviertel, Lower Austria, northwest of Vienna. Her father had been a peasant-farmer there. Thereafter, we more or less lose track of Maria Anna until, on 7 June 1837, the birth of her son Alois is entered in the Döllerheim parish register. How long she had been living there prior to the birth remains unknown, as do her whereabouts before coming to the village.

REALLY A ROTHSCHILD?

In the absence of more evidence, the scope for speculation is limitless:

Maria Anna's biography becomes a blank slate for scholarly speculation at its wildest. It is notoriously difficult to prove a negative. And who would want to, when it's so gratifying to our sense of historical *schadenfreude* to claim that the man responsible for the Holocaust was in some sense 'really' Jewish?

As early as the 1920s, there were rumours in Germany that Hitler's grandmother had, at the time of Alois's conception, been working in the Vienna household of Salomon Mayer von Rothschild, head of the Austrian branch of the famous banking dynasty. Eagerly as the story was retold, however, most acknowledged its unlikeliness even then: there's no supporting evidence for the claim.

THE FRANKENBERGER FACTOR

Then there is the appeal of the less outrageous argument that Hitler's father may have been a member of the Frankenberger (or Frankenreiter) family. In 1946, the Third Reich's former Minister of Justice, Hans Frank, revealed (drawing, he said, on evidence from Adolf's nephew Alphonse Hitler), that Alois's mother had worked as a cook in this bourgeois household in Graz, an important commercial city south of Vienna.

Family members had stayed in touch with Maria Anna for many years after she had left their service, even paying maintenance for her child. The conclusion some people drew is that the family cook must also have done service – whether willingly or reluctantly – as the lover of one of the family's men; most likely, Frank suggested, of the Frankenbergers' 19-year-old son.

Rural poverty in the nineteenth century was far from picturesque. Maria Anna Schicklgruber was born here, at Strones in Lower Austria.

political respectability and general integrity, Jetzinger's claims couldn't stand up. No record has been found of any Jewish family named Frankenberger or Frankenreiter living in Graz during the 1830s. (Nor was it likely: throughout this period, Jews were prohibited from living in that part of Austria. Hitler's Nuremberg Laws were only to be the latest in a very long line.) As seems to happen so often where the life and times of Adolf Hitler are concerned, what seems the most solid and authoritative of scholarly sources turns out to owe more to emotion than to fact.

SECRETS AND LIES

Maria Anna herself was to be no help to the historians of the future. For whatever reason, she would not reveal the identity of her baby's father, and Alois went down in the baptismal register as illegitimate. The obvious candidate for his paternity would seem to be Johann Georg Hiedler. However, this obviousness introduces additional doubt: if Johann Georg was Alois's father, and if he was to marry the boy's mother a few years later, why did he not marry her at the time?

The mundane truth may be that it wasn't deemed to matter much and that no enormous urgency was felt. Legitimacy was important, certainly, but its significance lay mainly in the fact that those born out of wedlock were not allowed to inherit property. Ultimately, it would

A sensational and opportunistic revelation, made in the context of Hans Frank's memoirs (written soon before his execution, and appropriately entitled *At the Gallows' Foot*), this story started to seem much more plausible when Franz Jetzinger revived it in the 1950s. The author of *Hitler's Youth* (1956), Jetzinger was no war criminal scrabbling to find favour with his captors, but a priest, a social democratic statesman, a civil servant and sometime librarian of Linz. It's scarcely surprising that this study should have caused a stir.

However, notwithstanding his clerical status, academic reputation,

matter a great deal to Alois, but as long as Johann Georg remained alive and in a position to save and spend his own money and dispose of his own property himself it very

likely didn't signify much either way.

There may, moreover, be less to these archival shenanigans than meets the eye. There's a striking casualness about the way the parish

priest in Döllerheim went about his work. A crude crossing out removed Alois's 'out of wedlock' status; the quickest of scribbles substituted 'within wedlock'. It's true that the writer signs his name (introducing the intriguing question of just how legally binding this 'legitimization' could really be), but it can hardly be claimed that he went to elaborate lengths to cover his tracks.

WHAT'S IN A NAME?

Another possibility is that Alois's uncle – Johann Georg's brother, Johann Nepomuk Hiedler (1807–8),who had no sons himself, and faced with the prospect of his family's surname disappearing – had demanded the change as the price of his dying legacy. That would offer another explanation of the late switch from Schicklgruber to Hitler. It also raises the question of why Alois didn't adopt Johann Nepomuk's favoured form of 'Hiedler', or the other versions he was known to use: 'Hüttler' or 'Huettler'. There is no contradiction, necessarily, between Alois's uncle's pride in his surname and his easy-going attitude to its spelling. Even so, it wraps what was already an enigma in another layer of mystery.

A further question could be posed: could Alois's 'uncle' have been his father all along? That leaves Johann Georg as nothing more than his brother's obliging or unwitting stand-in as Alois's parent,

Catholic piety marked Maria Anna's grave, as it appears to have imprinted her entire life. Her grandson would despise such simple faith.

Hans Frank (front left) served Hitler loyally as Justice Minister, but his post-war memoir served up little more than smears.

with Johann Nepomuk merely making him his legal heir when the time came. The truth is we don't know: there is no more evidence that Johann Nepomuk was Alois's father than that Baron Rothschild was – and there is no firm evidence that Johann Georg was, either.

A storm of confusion, secrecy and ignorance had formed round Adolf Hitler's antecedents even before he had been born. That confusion is only compounded by

our inability to truly understand the moral and social values of the time. Nineteenth-century Austria was unabashed about things we might have expected it to be more secretive about and yet a lot more exercised about issues that would not have worried us. If any of this is of more than academic importance, it may be because a sense of the dubiousness of his origins may have communicated itself to young Adolf, making him

more determined to forge and fulfil a destiny of his own.

LIKE FATHER...?
Whatever the doubts about his parentage, Alois's personal resolve was indisputable. He left school at 13, to be apprenticed to a cobbler, but he doesn't seem to have settled for this. Five years later, in 1855, availing himself of a government scheme that set out to recruit and train officials from the Empire's more far-flung corners, Alois was received into the imperial civil service. That he pursued this goal

A LEGITIMATE GRIEVANCE?

How far Alois can have felt any 'stain' of illegitimacy is debatable, and has accordingly been debated ferociously. In truth, however much a handicap 'bastard' status may have been from a legal point of view, it's by no means clear that it meant a moral mark of Cain.

Of 11 children, Maria Anna had been one of only six to survive into adulthood – nothing extraordinary by the standards of her social stratum, place and time. That sort of wastage helps explain what can in hindsight seem a surprisingly casual, pragmatic and even apparently permissive attitude to sex and parenthood in an otherwise conservative rural region, in an age we associate with repressively puritanical 'Victorian' values.

In Austria's small and scattered village communities, a nomadic population of male fieldhands came and went, according to the requirements of the seasons, from autumn ploughing to late summer harvest. Wealthier householders

lived cheek by jowl with an overwhelmingly female force of domestic servants, subject to seduction, sexual harassment and worse. Children were an inevitable by-product of this informal coming

and going and back-stairs hurly-burly. Out of sight and out of mind of government officials in Vienna, record-keeping was fairly notional; people learned not to enquire into their antecedents too closely.

Young Adolf would have seen this scowl routinely as a boy. His bastard status in some ways shaped his father Alois' life.

shows drive and determination, as did his slow and steady rise through the ranks of the bureaucracy.

But was this career to be a source of resentment, too? Alois was by no means unsuccessful. In 1892, he reached the rank of Higher

Collector of Customs – the highest position open to an official without a secondary education. This was an honourable post, and Alois's attainment of it was a respectable achievement, but it was also a reminder of how comparatively

low the ceiling was for someone of his background. A mandarin's pomp, an army of secretaries and clerks; the sumptuous carpeted and chandeliered office in Vienna … these were honours of which a man like him could only dream. Instead, over the course of 30 years, he was to be shunted from local post to local post, and his rise, although steady, was agonizingly slow.

Alois Schicklgruber left school at 13 to be apprenticed to a cobbler

If we want to, we can see a similarity between Alois's doggedness and that of his son, whose rise was also to take indomitable perseverance. But it may have been his bitter sense of grievance that communicated itself to his son; his sense of some vague but deep injustice to be righted – or even avenged. As yet, however, Alois's life as a family man lay some years off: he was more or less alone in the world as he made his way.

FAMILY MAN

Alois was not entirely solitary: he fathered an illegitimate child in the 1860s. But the fact that we know nothing about this infant, what became of the child, or even who its mother was, does not seem to suggest any deep or enduring attachment. Alois married for the first time in 1873,when he was 30 and his wife, Anna Glasl-Hörer, was 50 – and already ailing. Alois had married into the business, as it were – his wife was the daughter of a senior customs official. He appears

Alois cuts an impressive figure in his customs official's uniform, but his civil-service status was never more than lowly.

Big, bustling, vibrant Vienna is seen here in the 1860s when waltz-king Johann Strauss II wrote his 'By the Beautiful Blue Danube'.

AMBIGUOUS AUSTRIA

The geographical centre of Europe, Austria had for much of modern history been its powerful heart: the House of Habsburg had reigned over the Holy Roman Empire since medieval times. By the middle of the nineteenth century, however, that centrality had been called into question. Battered first by France under Napoleon and then by the Prussia of Wilhelm I and Bismarck, Austria had seen its authority progressively curtailed. By 1867, although still an imperial power, in partnership with the Crown of Hungary, its compromised status was evident in the hyphenated name of this new 'Austro-Hungarian Empire'.

Vienna was still the glittering capital of a rich and important state; Austrians could look back on a glorious imperial history. Increasingly, though, they were looking sideways, to the north and west, where a unified Germany was growing rapidly in power and influence.

On the throne since 1888, Kaiser Wilhelm II had been promising his subjects 'glorious times' – but no such prospects seemed in store for Austrians. German speakers themselves, they couldn't help hankering after membership of a brave new nation that was clearly on the rise, while Austria-Hungary was clearly fading. In northern Austria, where Alois spent so much of his life and where he eventually brought up his family, that impulse was especially strong: Germany felt much closer than Vienna there.

to have been briskly businesslike in his approach to the marriage: he certainly seems to have felt that a degree of freedom was written into his contract with Anna, to whom he was unfaithful from the start.

One of Alois's more persistent affairs was with the servant Franziska (or Fanni) Matzelsberger, who came to work in Alois's household in Braunau am Inn in 1876. Alois and Anna formally separated in 1880, whereupon Alois and Fanni started living as a married couple, although they weren't actually wed until a few months after Anna's death in 1883. By that time, Fanni had already borne Alois a son, also called Alois (1882–1956); a daughter, Angela, followed that July. Fanni quickly sickened in her turn, however. By August 1884 she too was dead and Alois was left a widower for a second time.

He did not stay single long. His third wife was already four months pregnant when she married Alois on 7 January 1885. Klara Pölzl (1860–1907) was the granddaughter of Johann Nepomuk Hiedler – Alois's uncle, and perhaps his father. That made them first cousins once

Hitler's half-brother, Alois Jr, lived in Liverpool, England, for some years, returning to Germany after World War I.

freakish, misbegotten monsters is hard to say. It does not seem to have outraged the Hitlers' own immediate community. In the comparatively small and isolated communities of provincial Europe at a time when travel and communications were not easy, men and women made the most of the social contacts they had at hand and the resulting relationships were not subjected to much scrutiny.

Alois's and Klara's wedding was mundane enough – not much more than a formality. A brief ceremony was held in Alois's home in Braunau am Inn before the start of an otherwise ordinary working day. Its main purpose, evidently, was to confer legitimacy on the baby son who was duly born that May.

Sadly, both Gustav and a younger sister Ida (born in September 1886) were to die of diphtheria in infancy. So too was a second son, Otto, born in 1887. Adolf was born 20 April 1889; a little brother, Edmund – born early in 1894 – was to die of measles six

removed at the very least. If Klara's grandfather Johann Nepomuk really *had* been her husband's father, they were niece and uncle – a kin-connection much too close for comfort. (Such a relationship would find an echo in the adult Adolf's relationship with his young half-niece Geli Raubal.)

The existence of the incest taboo is generally accounted for by the need for communities to prevent inbreeding and the reinforcement of unfortunate physical and mental traits to which this can lead. That being the case, it isn't difficult to see why Alois's and Klara's relationship should have been a focus for scholarly speculation. Adolf Hitler was so extravagantly evil, we can't help casting far and wide for an explanation. But whether his parents' coupling was really 'incestuous' enough for us to characterize its offspring as

Klara's face was striking only for its 'beautifully expressive' eyes: for her son, though, she represented an ideal of mother-love.

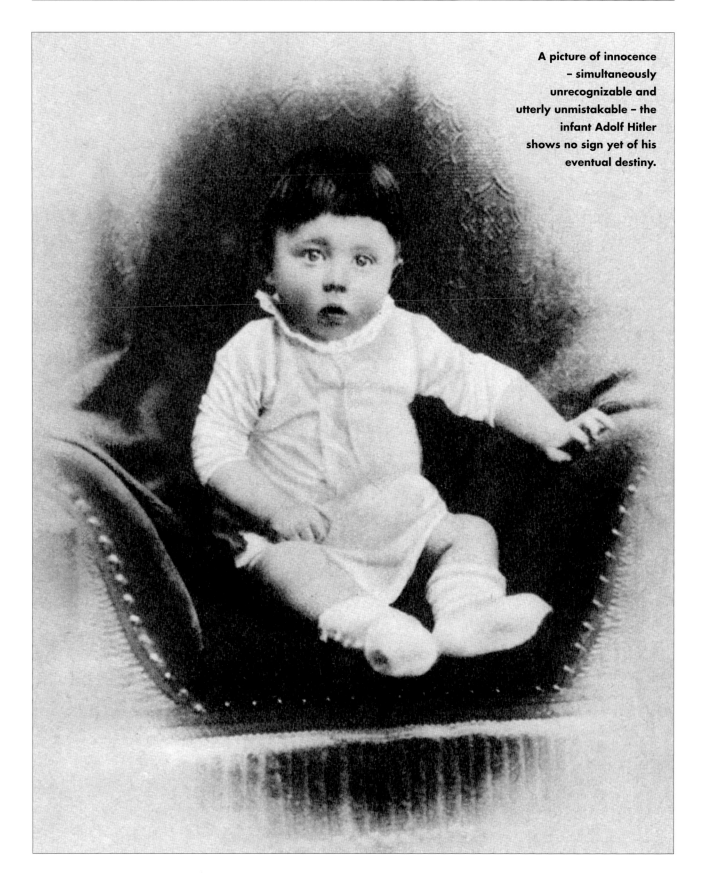

A picture of innocence – simultaneously unrecognizable and utterly unmistakable – the infant Adolf Hitler shows no sign yet of his eventual destiny.

AN HONORARY ARYAN?

'If all Jews were like him, there would be no Jewish question,' wrote Adolf Hitler to the *Anschluss* authorities in Austria. Eduard Bloch's impression that his patient Klara Hitler's son had been 'enormously grateful' for the care he'd taken was to prove justified in later years. In 1938, as anti-Semitism strengthened its hold upon the country, Bloch was to write to Germany's *Führer* to ask for his protection – and to receive it.

By no means the first bigot, nor the last, to make an exception of an individual known to him, Hitler threw all pseudo-scientific consistency to the winds in conferring on his

old family doctor the status of *edeljude*, or 'noble Jew'. Whether this willingness to exempt Eduard Bloch from his general denunciation of the Jews should be regarded as a redemptive glimmer of compassion or as confirmation of the vast irrationality of the Final Solution, it certainly benefited Bloch and his family. First shielded as Linz's other Jews were attacked, then spared when the rest of their community was rounded up and transported, they were given special permission to leave in 1940 and to find safe sanctuary in New York. Eduard died there, of stomach cancer, in 1945.

Eduard Bloch and his family were protected by Hitler.

years later. Adolf's only surviving full-sibling was his sister Paula (1896–1960). Could this sad succession of infant deaths be the result of inherited weaknesses, underlined by inbreeding? It seems possible – but then again, infant mortality was very high at the time.

MOTHER'S BOY

Whatever the cause of this cruel wastage, it was inevitable that the family's doctor would get to know the Hitlers well. Eduard Bloch (1872–1945) was to become an important source on Adolf's early background and biography, and about the only source we have on Klara – to Bloch a 'simple, modest,

kindly woman'. Although she was tall, he reports, her appearance could otherwise hardly have been more nondescript, given the 'brownish hair which she kept neatly plaited', and a 'long, oval face' that was made memorable by 'beautifully expressive grey-blue eyes'.

Bloch described the relationship between Klara and Adolf as loving and affectionate on the mother's side and devoted and deep-running on her son's. 'Outwardly,' he would remember later, 'his love for his mother was his most striking feature. Though he wasn't a mother's boy in the usual sense, I have never witnessed a closer

attachment.' During the illness that marked Klara's later years, young Adolf slept in the room next door to his mother, Bloch tells us. Although she was stoical herself, her sufferings 'seemed to torture her son'. The man who was subsequently to be seen as the very embodiment of sociopathy showed something very like empathy as he watched his mother waste away and die. 'An anguished grimace would come over him when he saw pain contract her face. There was little that could be done. An

Opposite: Bullied by her brother just as he was by his father, Paula seems to have forgiven him in later life.

injection of morphine from time to time would give temporary relief; but nothing lasting. Yet Adolf seemed enormously grateful even for these short periods of his release.'

ON THE MOVE

The life of a customs clerk like Alois could hardly have been characterized as romantic or adventurous, but he and his young family were nevertheless frequently on the move. In 1892, when Adolf was three, they moved across the border into Germany (Lower Bavaria), where Alois took up a post in Passau. As we have seen, the rank of Higher Collector of Customs was the highest position open to an official who had completed only elementary schooling, so Alois could justly feel pride in what he had achieved in the 30-odd years of his imperial service.

Another way of looking at it, though, is that Alois had taken an awfully long time to progress a comparatively short way up the official hierarchy. More to the point, he had come as far as he was ever going to – and he knew it. If the archetypal toddler grows up in an environment of optimism – his or her 20-something parents full of energy and hope – the first thing of which Adolf Hitler would have been conscious in his home life would have been his elderly father's frustrated realization that his long and slow career ascent had hit a dead end.

Was it Alois's sense of being marooned professionally that drove his restlessness about where

In this well-known class photo from 1899, 10-year-old Adolf already displays a certain dominant and assured presence.

Adolf was born in Alois' flat in this building in Braunau am Inn. Many want this historical legacy to be pulled down.

he lived? Granted, he was moved around from post to post, but his family was more nomadic than it need have been. There are believed to have been several moves within Passau even before Alois was transferred to Linz in April 1894. For the moment, Klara, Adolf and the infant Edmund stayed on in Passau.

We can only imagine this was a welcome respite for Klara and Adolf, given the toxic atmosphere that seems to have prevailed in their home. Alois's parenting style seems to have been of a piece with his irritable and domineering personality, and he took out his various resentments on his meek, submissive wife.

In February 1895, the family was unhappily reunited when they moved to Hafeld, Fischiham, near Lambach. The young Adolf started school there that May. A few weeks later, Alois retired, to spend much of his time pursuing his hobby of beekeeping. In 1897, the family moved to Lambach itself, moving within that city at the start of 1898 before a further move to Leonding, outside Linz, a few months later. Linz was to be the nearest thing Adolf Hitler had to a hometown.

There were plenty of sorrows in store, however: on 2 February 1900, Edmund died. Adolf's

progression to secondary school – to Linz's *Realschule* – that autumn must have felt like a mixed blessing: not yet in his teens, he was officially more educated than his thwarted father. Alois seems to have redoubled his efforts to exercise his influence on his son: some time around 1902, he took him into Linz's Customs Office in hopes of inspiring him. The visit had quite the opposite effect.

WHERE THERE'S A WILL
Just as Alois dealt out beatings to his wife and son, young Adolf persecuted Paula. 'The terror of

29

LINZ, A *FÜHRER* CITY

The capital of Upper Austria, Linz has long had a sense of its own importance, as perhaps befits the home of what is reputedly the oldest cake in world baking history, the latticed *Linzer Torte*. It has enjoyed more conventional prestige as well, being for a time in the Middle Ages the leading city of the Holy Roman Empire. Frederick III made his home here in the fifteenth century. Admittedly, that moment quickly came and went – Linz was soon surpassed in size and splendour by Vienna and by Budapest. But Linz retained a certain aura of prestige.

Klara's flat at Humboldtstrasse 31 was in the heart of town, just a stone's throw from the Hauptplatz, with its city hall, from whose balcony on the evening of 12 March 1938, after the *Anschluss*, an exultant *Führer* would proclaim the beginnings of his German Reich.

Hitler had big plans for his hometown. After his triumphant victory in the war, he envisaged, it would have been one of the five great '*Führer* Cities' whose scale and magnificence would proclaim his glory to the world. Buoyed up by industrial and economic growth, it was destined to double in size. There would be splendid homes for its leading citizens and a collection of impressive public buildings, including a stadium, a party headquarters and

educational institutions (including an observatory whose astronomical research would help explode the 'pseudo-science of the Catholic Church').

In the event, Linz was largely flattened in the fighting, losing 12,000 buildings in 200 air raids between 1944 and the conclusion of the war. Not just the home of

Linz was a handsome town. Hitler's pride in the place is understandable.

Hitler's schooldays, but a few years later that of Adolf Eichmann, who had helped Hitler in his designs for the Final Solution, the city made strenuous efforts to 'de-Nazify' in the post-war era. Investigations were conducted into the recent past, once-secret records were released to public view, and memorials established to commemorate those killed. Although its Hitlerian heritage may have been a mixed blessing, Linz remains an attractive cultural city, now emerging as a centre for new media.

LIVING SPACE

'Imagine…' Hitler was later to invite the reader of *Mein Kampf*:

In a basement apartment, consisting of two stuffy rooms, dwells a worker's family of seven. Among the five children there is a boy of, let us assume, three years. This is the age in which the first impressions are made on the consciousness of the child. Talented persons retain traces of memory from this period down to advanced old age. The very narrowness and overcrowding of the room does not lead to favorable conditions. Quarreling and wrangling will very frequently arise as a result. In these circumstances, people do not live with one another, they press against one another.…

Among the children, of course, this is still bearable; they always fight under such circumstances, and among themselves they quickly and thoroughly forget about it. But if this battle is carried on between the parents themselves, and almost every day in forms which for vulgarity often leave nothing to be desired, then, if only very gradually, the results of such visual instruction must ultimately become apparent in the children. The character they will inevitably assume if this mutual quarrel takes the form of brutal attacks of the father against the mother, of drunken beatings, is hard for anyone who does not know this milieu to imagine. At the age of six the pitiable little boy suspects the existence of things which can inspire even an adult with nothing but horror.

Although Alois was not a 'worker', nor his house a 'basement apartment' nor home to seven, it is still difficult, given what we know, to see this situation as being quite as hypothetical as Hitler says. No dwelling could have been big enough to give Klara and her children the emotional space they would have needed to come through the patriarchal tyranny of Alois unscathed.

Even if we take Hitler's description here at face value, it is fairly grim. If, as Gertrud Kurth suggests, we look more closely into phrases like 'forms which for vulgarity often leave nothing to be desired', 'hard for anyone who does not know the milieu to imagine' or 'things which can inspire even an adult with nothing but horror' – it's hard to resist the sense that Hitler is hinting at something much more serious and sinister. Some have found a suggestion of child sex abuse in this passage; at the least, it seems, there is the 'brutal' violence of the father against the mother.

Did Hitler's later concept of geopolitical *lebensraum* – the idea that Germany had a duty to expand its territories eastward into the lands of the Slavs to give itself more 'living space' – originate in a young boy's horrified feelings for his family and fears for his mother?

the Third Reich was cultivated in Hitler's own home,' historian Florian Beierl has claimed. No one would dispute that life under Alois's roof was grim. But the gap between the father's domestic

tyranny and the national and geopolitical domination his son was ultimately able to exercise is clearly vast – and unhappy homes like the Hitlers' are all too commonplace. Witnesses agree, however, that the violent oppressiveness he witnessed must have affected the young Adolf badly, especially as he grew older and felt the need to try to protect his mother. And he did protect her up to a point: the defiance he

A single student separates future philosopher Ludwig Wittgenstein (second-back row, third from right) from future *Führer* Adolf Hitler (back row, far right).

showed in the face of his father's attacks upon the helpless Klara were widely remarked upon; he does not seem to have been short of courage when it counted.

Could it have been these childhood circumstances that brought Hitler to the view that true heroism was to be found in indomitable resistance? In later life, he was, notoriously, to formulate a doctrine of the supremacy of the 'will' that he had found in his readings of Friedrich Nietzsche (1844–1900) and Martin Heidegger (1889–1976). As J.P. Stern has pointed out, the *Führer* took with fatuous literalism an idea that those philosophers had advanced much more metaphorically. It is nevertheless intriguing that Hitler latched on to this particular aspect of their work. He could certainly stick to his guns – and did so even in his early adolescence when he stood out against his father's urgings to join the civil service.

Hitler was later to insist that, even now, he knew he wanted to be an artist. There is no substantive evidence to support this claim, but there is testimony that he constantly and fearlessly enraged Alois with his refusal to submit.

OLD SCHOOL TIES

This talk of Nietzsche and Heidegger takes us to Ludwig Wittgenstein (1889–1951). The famous philosopher was a schoolmate of Adolf's at the *Realschule* in Linz. In strict chronological terms, the two were almost exact contemporaries: born on 26 April 1889, Wittgenstein was Hitler's junior by just six days. However, as the precocious Wittgenstein was moved up a grade and Hitler held back, they were two full school years apart. How much they would have seen each other from day to day, or whether they would have had any reason to interact, is unclear. This could simply be a curious coincidence.

Sometime schoolmate Ludwig Wittgenstein was to follow a very different path from Hitler, becoming one of the greatest philosophers of his age.

The Hitlers' home in Leonding, where Adolf's conflict with his father reached its height. They fought over the future direction of his life.

Kimberley Cornish is not convinced: he argues in his study *The Jew of Linz* (1998) that the conflict between the two was a turning point in Hitler's life and in his formation as an anti-Semite. It's certainly true that the future dictator would have had (or felt he had) grounds for resentment towards young Wittgenstein, the scion of a wealthy and influential local family. It's true too that he had three Jewish grandparents – although, significantly, these didn't include his maternal grandmother; and both his mother and his father identified as Roman Catholics.

The link is intriguing, and it is difficult to resist the temptation to make something of this potential link between two of the twentieth century's most commanding personalities. But despite their period of close proximity, there is no real evidence that they ever met one another, let alone that they were involved in any classroom confrontation or schoolyard brawl.

Granted, despite his distance, Wittgenstein would have been a recognizable figure around the school: he stood out on the one hand with his academic brilliance; on the other with his shy sensitivity and stammering speech – frequently the object of unpleasant teasing. But there is no obvious reason why he and Adolf Hitler would have been thrown together in the everyday run of *Realschule* life. Nor is it clear that Hitler would have known that his smarter schoolmate was 'Jewish' (which technically he wasn't – although he would have been by Hitler's later racial standards). The link proves something of a dead end. 'Whereof one cannot speak; thereof one must be silent,' runs one of Wittgenstein's most celebrated observations. This would seem to be one of those things.

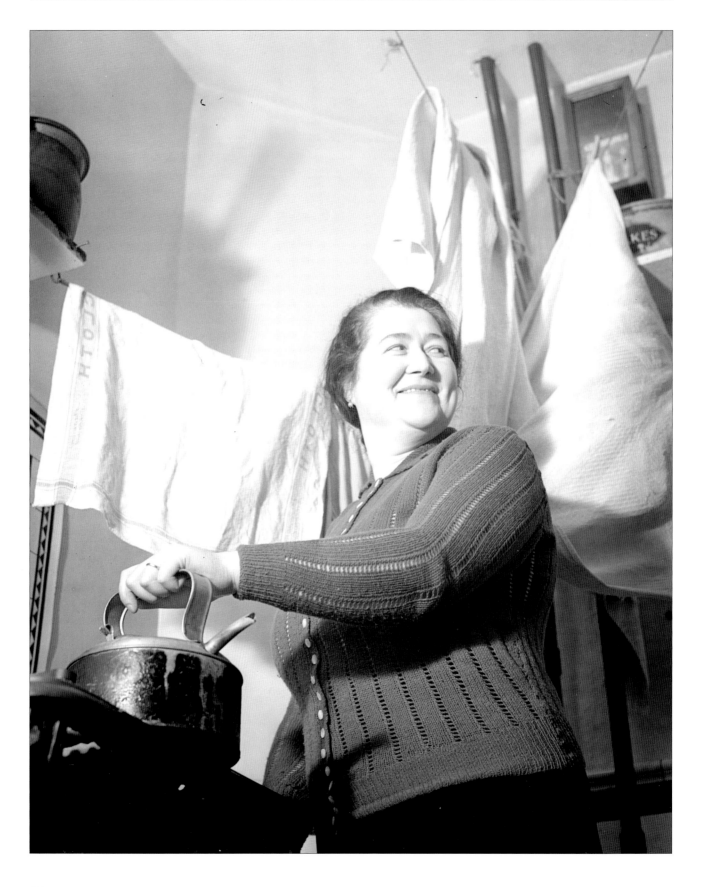

AN EDUCATION IN OBSTINACY

If Hitler's time at school was truly formative, it is unlikely to have been on account of any single incident or conflict. More significant, perhaps, would have been the more or less constant humiliation inherent in being a boy who dreamed of greatness and glory on the back of merely average intelligence and what seems likely to have been less than average academic focus and application.

The determination needed to defy his father seems to have fostered in young Adolf an (in some ways) admirable, enabling, yet ultimately deceptive and destructive self-belief. There is no direct evidence to support this surmise. There is much evidence, though, that in later years, at the height of his power and in the most crucial crises of his leadership, he was to have a short attention span and an inability to take even constructive criticism or advice when it mattered most.

THE GERMAN QUESTION

One man who, by Hitler's own enthusiastic testimony, did exercise an influence on him at Linz's *Realschule* was his history teacher, Leopold Poetsch (1853–1942). Clearly a character, individual enough to stand out in the memory of an adolescent boy, but typical too of his nationality and of his age and its assumptions, Poetsch was a native of Sankt Andrä, in southern Austria. He had, however, had his first teaching position in Maribor,

Opposite: Alois Jr did his bit to make the Hitler family more multicultural when he married Dubliner Bridget Dowling in 1910 (shown here in 1941).

Dated 2 February, 1900, this certificate confirmed young Adolf Hitler's rights as a member of the community of Linz.

now Slovenia, an area whose German inhabitants at this time found themselves confronting a rise in 'Pan-Slavic' consciousness.

Local Slavs saw themselves as part of a wider national movement uniting peoples from Slovakia to Russia and from Bulgaria to Poland. A comparable renaissance had been gaining force among Slovenia's Hungarian and Romanian minorities. This kind of nationalism had been on the rise for decades across much of central Europe: its supreme achievement had arguably been the unification of Germany itself, under Otto von Bismarck (1815–98). Down here in the southern Slavic marches, though, German dominance seemed genuinely insecure – an affront to so proud a patriot as Poetsch.

Poetsch mythologized the Germanic strand in Austria's history in heroic terms

---

His response seems to have been to mythologize Germany's history and the Germanic strand in Austria's; to reimagine these in heroic terms, gathering all their various vicissitudes into an extended epic of national self-realization.

It is hard to know now how much of what Hitler thought he remembered from Poetsch's classes

was owed to Poetsch himself and how much to his own highly coloured historical imagination. There is no doubt, though, that he found these lessons inspirational. 'Even today,' he was to recall a decade later in *Mein Kampf* (1925), 'I think back with gentle emotion on this grey-haired man who, by the fire of his narratives, sometimes made us forget the present; who, as if by enchantment, carried us into past times and, out of the millennial veils of mist, moulded dry historical memories into living reality. On such occasions we sat there, often aflame with enthusiasm, and sometimes even moved to tears.'

Poetsch didn't just evoke a glorious past: he used it explicitly politically, to point up parallels in the Austria and Germany of the day:

'What made our good fortune all the greater was that this teacher knew how to illuminate the past by examples from the present, and how from the past to draw inferences

The Brothers Grimm found in folktales the basis for a new and powerful sense of German nationhood.

the systemizing, regularizing tendencies of the Enlightenment and the eighteenth century's 'Age of Reason', poets and artists had sought to set free the human spirit in all its passion and creativity. Much of that creativity was to be unleashed by the contemplation of Nature in all its splendour; the sense of the rural landscape as a cradle – and, it seemed to follow, the nation as a home.

The movement's influence in Germany could be traced in everything from the poems of Goethe to *Grimm's Fairy Tales*. Putting Germany, and the German language, on the literary map of Europe, the works of Wolfgang Johann von Goethe (1749–1832) had helped to foster a new sense of German pride. The Brothers Grimm (Jacob, 1785–1863 and Wilhelm, 1786–1859) collected folktales in the farthest-flung and most isolated corners of the countryside. Firmly rooted in tradition and comparatively untouched by literary convention, these tales seemed to represent German culture in something like a 'natural' state.

The progressive unification of the country over the course of the nineteenth century was reflected in the work of poets such as Heinrich von Kleist (1777–1811) and Heinrich Heine (1797–1856). Composers such as Franz Schubert (1797–1828) and Robert Schumann (1810–56) didn't just boost German prestige with the praise their music garnered internationally: the songs

for the present. As a result he had more understanding than anyone else for all the daily problems which then held us breathless. He used our budding nationalistic fanaticism as a means of educating us, frequently appealing to our sense of national honor.'

The naked partisanship of Poetsch's teaching seems shocking today, but it evidently didn't dismay Hitler. Hardly surprising, perhaps,

given the casual, essentially approving way in which he refers to his own and his fellow students' 'fanaticism' at this time.

ROMANTIC STIRRINGS

Herr Poetsch was not alone in his romancing of the German past: small-n nationalism had been a hallmark of the Romantic movement in Europe as a whole. In powerful reaction to

or *lieder* they wove around poetic lyrics promoted German literature and myth around the world.

But the sort of 'nationalism' these writers and composers represented did not generally extend much beyond a basic pride in the German homeland, its natural beauty, its history and its culture, and in the German language and the literature to which it had given rise. It was a patriotic pride, for sure, and German writers referred without embarrassment to the 'Fatherland' – this word did not as yet connote anything beyond a sense of love and trust and familial belonging.

WAGNERIAN AWAKENING

So far, so understated – so eminently reasonable, indeed. The situation was transformed when Richard Wagner (1813–83) burst on to the German scene. Although his works are loosely described as 'operas', he saw them as 'musical theatre' – an utterly immersive, sensually exhilarating and emotionally explosive experience of music, scenery, symbolic imagery and speech. This wonderfully talented composer reached back into ancient folk tradition for his subject matter; he evoked a world of warrior-heroes, maiden princesses and mythic spirits. Above all, it was a *Germanic* world, in which the idea of the homeland took on an almost mystic sanctity and in which its enemies were seen as devilish monsters, dwarves – or Jews.

In Wagner, who had grown up nursing who-knows-what resentments from a boyhood in Leipzig's Jewish quarter and an early career in what he saw as a Jewish-dominated German music scene, anti-Semitic prejudice had attained a pretty much unprecedented level. The power and pettiness of his hatred can hardly be overstated. In his works, though – in great operas like *Lohengrin* (1850), *The Mastersingers of Nuremberg* (1868), *Parsifal* (1882), and the sequence *The Ring of the Nibelung* (1876) – racist venom is transmuted into music at its most sublime. Wagner, regardless of his faults, was a composer of great genius. Not just that, but his works are peculiarly arresting. With their endless melodies – each song, each scene spilling over into the next; their eerie harmonies; their sumptuous orchestrations; they don't just delight the mind but transport the soul.

Richard Wagner's ravishing music caught the young Hitler in its spell – as did the rabid anti-Semitism which went with it.

Seen live, as Wagner intended (he took a strong interest in everything from the libretto to the scenery in his dramas), their impact can be overwhelming. It is not difficult to see why these works would have had an arresting effect on a young, impressionable and obviously imaginative boy: Hitler claims to have seen his first performance of *Lohengrin* at the age of 12. 'In one instant, I was addicted,' he recalled. 'My youthful enthusiasm … knew no bounds.' For once, the metaphor of addiction does not

> ## *Wagner's works had an arresting effect on the young, impressionable Adolf*

seem excessive. A single viewing of *Tristan und Isolde* (1859) can change lives. Over the next few years, however, Hitler was to see this supreme celebration of tragic love no fewer than 40 times. He was eating, sleeping and

breathing Wagner and his works. He read the composer's published essays voraciously – taking their rambling, ranting sentences for true philosophy. Wagner's thinking, he would later say, 'is intimately familiar to me. At every stage of my life I come back to him.'

There can be no doubt that Hitler's love of Wagner helped to feed and shape his anti-Semitism. It may have inspired him politically as well. Wagner's was not just a musical but a totalizing vision, appealing to every sense and encompassing every aspect of artistic appreciation. Hitler's ultimate ambition was not just to be

Love, death and self-sacrifice come ecstatically together at the climactic end of Wagner's *Tristan und Isolde*.

SCAPEGOATING THE JEWS

Jew-hatred was nothing new in Germany – any more than it was in the rest of Europe. In medieval times, the Jews had been persecuted as alien infidels – as the 'Killers of Christ'. This was one pre-Reformation prejudice that Martin Luther (1483–1546) had enthusiastically embraced, and one he made sure remained at the heart of German Protestantism. In the nineteenth century, however, as Romantic patriotism began to gel with self-consciously modern and purportedly 'scientific' racial theories, anti-Semitism took a new and disturbing turn.

Christoph Meiners (1747–1810) was an early example: a product of the European Enlightenment, he'd tried to examine racial differences as clearly and dispassionately as a naturalist might study animal or plant species. A polygenist, he believed that the different races sprang from completely different origins. As so often when a supposedly scientific approach is insufficiently sophisticated in its understanding or rigorous in its method, however, he brought many subjective assumptions to his 'objective' view.

Hence he concluded that Black Africans had smaller brains than Caucasians. Hence too his confident assertion that the Slavs belonged to a 'lower' race than Western European: like the Asiatic races, they were more limited in their mental capacities.

Meiners' was just one of many 'scientific' theories in its day. Not until the late nineteenth century were such views becoming mainstream. That they did was in large part a result of the need to justify the great European colonial project. Take Meiners' view that Black Africans had 'thick nerves'

that quite literally dulled their feelings, reducing their sensitivity to pain – a clear pass for the conscience of the slave-owner and the overseer with his whip. Long before this, however, the emotional basis of this sort of racial prejudice had been set in place by the myth-making works of artists, poets and musicians – above all those of Richard Wagner.

It appears to have been him, in fact, who characterized the very existence of the Jews as 'the Jewish Problem', and who looked to their eradication as the 'Final Solution'. They were, Wagner said, 'the born enemy of pure humanity and everything noble in it'. In a declining, degenerate world in which heroism was history and true patriotic and personal feeling dead, Wagner insisted, the money-grabbing, treacherous, cynical Jews held sway.

a successful statesman but a sort of super-impresario, re-presenting and re-orchestrating an entire nation. With its swastikas, banners and big parades, Nazism would not just be an ideology: it would be a new aesthetic; a new way of responding to the world.

A HOLY FAMILY?

Hitler's religious adherences and their part in his wider moral, political and social beliefs were one day to be a focus for heated debate. How far it can be said to have shaped his views must be

very doubtful, but for what it is worth, he had a strongly Catholic upbringing.

Klara was deemed devout even by the standards of the time. Embarrassed apologists point – with justice – to his father's outspoken anti-clericalism. It remains the case, however, that this sort of division of spiritual labour within the family is a Catholic cliché. Whatever airs he liked to give himself as a self-consciously intellectual critic of priestly authority, Alois tacitly backed his wife in the religious upbringing

she gave her children. So Adolf underwent all the usual sacraments of baptism, first communion and confirmation as a boy.

In January 1903, his family was hit by Alois's death: however abusive he had been, the shock of his departure must have had an impact. It is hard to delineate its effects: certainly, Adolf's exam results at school that year showed neither a freshly liberated 'bounce' nor a slump of grief. No such slump was necessary for the underachieving Adolf to fail once more and be held back another

Opposite: Hitler's visits to his parents' grave in the town cemetery at Leonding became part of National Socialist ceremonial.

Right: Alois and Klara Hitler's tomb remained an important shrine for neo-Nazis until its eventual removal in 2012.

year as contemporaries moved on. We cannot easily account for Hitler's slowness at school. Was that 'unsatisfactory' in French down to patriotic obstinacy or academic weakness? If the latter, was it the result of a native lack of intellectual capacity or of the (understandable) disaffection of a boy from an abusive home? Whatever the reason, in 1904, his mother moved him to the *Realschule* at Steyr, which was far enough away for him to have to board. His results remained mediocre, however.

AFTER ALOIS

Hitler could come home in the holidays to a surprisingly large and impressive flat in the city centre to which his mother had moved in the aftermath of Alois's death. In later life, in self-mythologizing spirit, Hitler would point to the wretchedness of his upbringing; up to a point, this was true. But Alois's anger and irritability – and the violence these caused, and the unhappiness attendant on that – had never had their origin in material poverty as such. Despite his lowly official rank, Alois had inherited some modest degree of wealth – hence the ability of his widow, a sometime servant, to set up home in Humboldtstrasse. If her husband had not given her much

of a life, he had provided well for her in his passing: Klara and her children could live the life of the bourgeoisie.

And, like a true scion of that class, Hitler could afford to take his time about important life decisions. Although during his stay at Steyr he got his grades up sufficiently to

graduate and – in theory, at least – to go on to a technical college, he found it more comfortable to stay at home with Klara. And that is what he did, from late 1905 to 1907: a period with no obvious achievements to show for it, but a period of preparation, he insisted, for his life as a great artist.

had never been in doubt: the Academy's examiners had havered only over his *possible* potential as an architect. (Quite a few of Hitler's paintings that have survived have buildings as their subjects.) By Hitler's own admission, he had obdurately resisted the instruction in mathematics that the *Realschule* had offered him, leaving himself

Below: Hitler's paintbox went with him everywhere. Here it is authenticated in a letter by the US officer who captured it in 1945.

poorly placed to pursue an architectural training now.

Injury and insult were alike redoubled, when, refusing to take no for an answer, Hitler applied again the following year: the Academy seems to have given him still shorter shrift. This reapplication and its ignominious outcome seem promptly to have been banished from Hitler's memory; they had no place in his later memoirs. At the time it must have stung, however – especially when it came so hard upon the death of his dear mother. Klara had died in December 1907, a few weeks after his first rejection. By the end of 1908, Hitler had lost both his lifelong comfort and – it was starting to appear – his lifelong ambition. Where in the world was he supposed to go from here?

The answer was simple: Vienna, where he'd been intending to go in any case, if – or, rather, when (as he imagined was inevitable) – the Academicians said 'Yes'. Hitler had already realized the importance of persistence. 'I went to Vienna with a suitcase,' he would write in *Mein Kampf*, 'containing some clothes and my linen, in my hand, and an unshakeable determination in my heart.' A melodramatic opening to this new chapter? 'Years of Study and Suffering', he was to call

Right: A watercolour from the 1900s displays the artist's talent – and his limitations. A nicely executed but uninspiring (and oddly unpeopled) scene.

his account of the next few years. The self-dramatizing tone may seem exaggerated, but it wasn't wholly unwarranted. As a solitary, self-funded incomer struggling

to make it on his own, Hitler was certainly to find things very different from the calm routine and orderly progression he might have expected in the Academy.

THE AUSTRIAN COSMOPOLIS

Hitler was to find Vienna very different from his cherished ideal of the German city: a multi-ethnic melting pot (Hitler himself preferred to call Austria-Hungary a 'porridge of nations') for an extraordinarily diverse and complex empire. German was just one of many languages to be heard on its

'TOO FEW HEADS'

Later critics have queued up to deride the drawings and paintings of the youthful Hitler. And fair enough: he was by no means the genius he thought he was. It is hard to avoid a suspicion, though, that they're protesting too much in their gleeful vindictiveness. More broadly, too, the reluctance to concede that a man universally acknowledged as a moral monster might also have some degree of artistic talent suggests a certain confusion over what creative inspiration is.

The instant dismissal of Hitler's works is arguably unfortunate, too, in closing off what might be an avenue of understanding: a window on the consciousness (and subconscious) of the man. The judges at the Academy notoriously noted that his works showed 'too few heads' – a technical challenge

ducked, they seem to have thought. But if it's true that the surviving works we have are strikingly 'unpeopled', could the explanation lie somewhere deeper – maybe darker – in the artist's soul?

Signed 'Hitlers' sell at upwards of $100,000 now – not, though, for their value as works of art.

It's curious, too, that Hitler's 'failure' seems to some extent to have been self-decided. The Vienna Academy was internationally renowned. Did their rejection really add up to a final, definitive, thumbs down for the young artist? Was there really no scope for his talent to be developed or improved? It is revealing, perhaps, that while he was prepared to persist in – even, in some ways, to suffer for – his art, Adolf doesn't seem to have explored alternative routes, perhaps through less prestigious schools. It was 'greatness' or nothing, apparently; Hitler had no doubt of his destiny or of his ability to attain glory through sheer force of will.

streets, struggling to be heard above the babel of Hungarian, Croatian, Romanian, Slovene and Czech.

Fresh as he was from the quiet and calm of Linz, so abruptly bereft of Klara's affection and support, it's hardly surprising that Hitler should have found the city intimidating. Fewer than half the population was Vienna-born, making this the ultimate modern city – vast and anonymous. People came and went unnoticed: a general sense of transience and provisionality reigned. Hence the city's appeal to foreign fugitives such as the Russian revolutionaries Leon Trotsky and Joseph Stalin. (Their

stays in Vienna seem, intriguingly, to have overlapped with Hitler's, though there is no evidence that the Russians and the Austrian ever met.) But this mongrel identity was the last thing to recommend Vienna to someone who, however strong his yearnings for metropolitan success and world renown, missed his mother – and the intimate security of his hometown.

It would have been a grave affront to Herr Poetsch's student to find his German language and heritage just one of many competing cultures here. Worst of all, though, was the presence – and the unabashed self-confident

presence – of a significant population of Jews. 'One day when I was walking through the inner city,' Hitler confides to his reader in *Mein Kampf*, 'I suddenly came upon a being clad in a long caftan, with black curls.

'Is this also a Jew? was my first thought.

'At Linz they certainly did not look like that. Secretly and cautiously I watched the man, but the longer I stared at this strange face and scrutinized one feature after the other, the more my mind reshaped the first question into another form:

'Is this also a German?'

READING REINFORCEMENT

To point to the anti-Semitism implicit in the description and in the rhetorical questions it prompts would seem redundant. More interesting, perhaps, is our young protagonist's response:

'As was my custom in such cases, I tried to remove my doubts by reading.'

'Reading' for information and enlightenment would appear sensible; commendable indeed. But it is perhaps perverse to read to 'remove [one's] doubts'. That Hitler meant to do exactly that is underlined by his choice of reading matter: 'For the first time in my life I bought some anti-Semitic pamphlets,' he reveals. This seems to have been his approach to reading all the way through these 'years of study' – and, indeed, in later years when he assembled an impressive-looking library as his country's *Führer*.

Pamphlets apart, he wasn't to run short of reading matter. No one in the German-speaking Central Europe of the early twentieth century was likely to. Even as no more than an anonymous bystander, the young Hitler had arrived in Vienna just as it was in the throes of an exciting and dramatic intellectual revolution.

As the example of Wagner reminds us, though, genius can come with some unseemly baggage. This was a golden age with a gamey side, bringing together the sublime and the squalid; brute prejudice and hate with transcendent beauty. Its ambivalence was perhaps best exemplified in the writings of the

This barn is almost interesting: it's easy to see why the Vienna examiners thought Hitler might just make it as an architect.

age's leading philosopher, Friedrich Nietzsche – as exhilarating as they were outrageous; even perilous, perhaps.

THE END OF TRUTH

'Above all, do not mistake me for someone else!' Nietzsche demanded of the readers of his *Ecce Homo*. But he was constantly to be misrepresented and misunderstood. Not surprisingly, it has to be said, given the abstruseness of his writings on being and on epistemology (the nature of knowledge). In Nietzsche's final years, the extravagance of his ideas gave way to the literal incoherence of madness, but by that time he'd left Western thought as utterly bewildered as he was himself. Nietzsche poured

eloquent and irrefutably articulate scorn on all existing philosophies of existence – and on the moral codes to which they gave rise. His attack left the whole field of philosophical

enquiry so much scorched earth.

How, he asked, could we claim realistically to have any sort of access to the 'truth' when that truth could be expressed only in the

Opposite: Austria's Academy of Fine Arts, his country's cultural stronghold, at whose imposing doors young Hitler was to knock in vain.

words and ideas that were already available to us – and that were only capable of coming up with the same pre-set solutions? Philosophical investigation was thus condemned to an endless – and ultimately pointless – circularity. 'When someone hides something behind a bush', he drily observed, 'and looks for it in the same place and finds it again, there is not much praise to be had for such a "discovery".'

THE DEATH OF GOD

This insight did not just change philosophy but completely turned it upside down: it was not just that our beliefs were wrong but that

beliefs themselves were wrong. Nietzsche's claim that 'convictions are more dangerous enemies of truth than lies' followed logically – but it made a nonsense of the way we saw the world. So helpless was humankind in the face of such confusion; so utterly disorientated; so completely at sea; that it seemed the universal order was crumbling about our ears. 'God is dead,' said Nietzsche notoriously: all those universal structures that shaped our world, our experiences, were at their centre empty; there was no ordering authority to keep things in their place.

The idea of the 'death of God' was by no means new; it had existed for many decades, at least as an ironic epigram. The Enlightenment and the advent of modern science had seemingly

abolished all the certainties of the 'Age of Faith': a helpless humanity had been left existentially orphaned by their disappearance. Nietzsche took the idea much further, and expressed it much more memorably than it had been before, sketching out a shocking yet exhilarating vision of absurdity; a cataclysmic comedy of 'tragic laughter'.

THE BIRTH OF THE SUPERMAN

Having pronounced the deity dead, with a coroner's finality, Nietzsche set about supplanting his whole function as divinity with that of the 'Superman'. This being would provide for himself the values 'God' had done before. By an effort of sheer will, he would confer on his universe the meaning it would need to make some sort of sense, creating the laws by which he lived and the moral context in which he did so.

Published posthumously, in 1908, *Ecce Homo* amounts to

Hitler's sketchbook attests to the seriousness with which he pursued his vocation – and, perhaps, the pedestrian quality of this pursuit.

Those foundations were, he posited, the superior intelligence, talent and resourcefulness of the Aryan or white European nations – and especially the Nordic and Germanic Teutons. Conversely, these foundations were undermined by the pervasive influence of the Jews. The story of civilization, he said, was destined to culminate in a final and fatal confrontation between the forces of (Aryan) good and (Jewish) evil.

His ideology posited the superior intelligence, talent and resourcefulness of the Aryan nations

Inevitably, perhaps, when it was required to be one whole half of an all-encompassing duality, Chamberlain's definition of the 'Jew' was very wide. It included, for example, the Chinese. On the other hand, intrigued by linguistic and archaeological findings that a lighter-skinned 'Aryan' people from the western steppes had in late prehistoric times invaded the south Asian subcontinent and established themselves as its ruling Brahmin caste, he made a surprising exception for India. (Hence the popularity among his followers of the originally Hindu swastika symbol, which would one day be incorporated into the iconography of Nazism.)

Vienna in 1910 was among the biggest, most diverse and liveliest cities in the world.

A 'SCIENCE' OF SUPREMACY

Chamberlain's notions built on earlier work by thinkers such as Georges Buffon (1707–88), Petrus Camper (1722–89) and Germany's own Christoph Meiners. Count Georges Vacher de Lapouge (1854–1936) had raised these further. Writing with style and supreme confidence – and a dazzling appearance of deep learning – Chamberlain repackaged vulgar prejudice as seeming 'science'.

If his masterwork took the German home of the 'master race' by storm, it must be acknowledged that it appealed far more widely. All the white European nations found its conclusions flattering – the further north they hailed from, the more so, as a rule. *Foundations* was ecstatically received in England, whose proudly Anglo-Saxon elite were delighted to see their empire-builders' status justified; to have their 'right' to rule in Africa, India and other lands confirmed.

That prerogative was being busily exercised now by all the main European powers. The Berlin Conference of 1884 had sounded the start of a headlong 'Scramble for Africa'. In alliance with Austria-Hungary, Germany had been building an empire in the east of the continent, in Rwanda, Burundi and Tanzania; further south in Namibia, and in West Africa's Cameroon, Togo and Ghana.

CIVILIZATION AND SAVAGERY

Its real motivation may have been the competition for resources and strategic power, but the Scramble for Africa claimed a moral justification. The natives of the 'Dark Continent' needed European rule, conversion to Christianity and education in Western ways if they were to be raised up from the animal savagery in which they dwelt. Opportunistic it may have been, but the argument was generally persuasive to a European public for whom Africa's indigenous peoples, with their incomprehensible languages and customs, their dark skins and strangely textured hair, seemed strikingly alien – and self-evidently inferior.

The writings of Houston S. Chamberlain lent plausibility to prejudice; gave European chauvinism an air of academic truth.

The conflictual opposition between Europe and Africa/Asia appeared to be reflected analogously in those between 'civilization' and 'barbarism'; 'reason' and 'instinct'; 'human' and 'animal'. And, at least imaginatively, in that between a masculine principle that upheld order, discipline and manly restraint and a feminine one composed of unbridled feeling and desire.

Those principles warred in human society and culture – as indeed they did in the individual psyche as delineated by psychologists like Sigmund Freud. Psychoanalysis can in hindsight be seen as a sort of colonial settlement of this uncivilized subconscious: 'Where *id* was, there shall *ego* be,' Freud had said.

MOOD MUSIC

German culture in general had been rich in achievements in recent decades – most unproblematically, perhaps, in the area of classical music. Linz-born Anton Bruckner

Could Germans look like this? Hitler's suspicions of the Jews were widely shared, if seldom so strongly felt or extravagantly developed.

(1824–96) had set out to rival – and to challenge – the chaster classicism espoused by Johannes Brahms (1833–97), his vast and rambling symphonic works marked out by deep and lush harmonies. Intense emotion went hand and hand with artistic audacity in the works of Hugo Wolf (1860–1903), who

Representatives of the European powers came together at the Berlin Conference to carve up Africa into colonial territories.

invented the German *lied* for this new era. Although some despised him as a Jew, and his compositions struggled to find the acceptance they really merited, Gustav Mahler (1860–1911) still presided over the Viennese musical scene as a conductor.

Wagner's influence was immense, of course – most of all, perhaps, on the operas, songs and symphonies of Richard Strauss (1864–1949). No one did more to set the transgressive spirit of Friedrich Nietzsche to music than Strauss,

whose every work seemed more audacious than his last. In 1896, he published a tone poem based on the philosopher's masterwork, *Also Sprach Zarathustra* ('Thus Spake Zarathustra', 1891): 'the highest book there is,' its author maintained.

ROLLER CALL

We know that Hitler took an interest (or least aspired to) in things philosophical; his love of music – or at least of Wagner – is well documented. His declared ambition,

though, at this time of his life was to be an artist, and his first call on arriving in Vienna after his first rejection by the Academy appears to have been upon Alfred Roller (1864–1935). His late mother's landlady, Magdalena Hanisch, had given him a letter of introduction to Roller, a family friend of hers. Hitler, she assured him, was an 'earnest, aspiring young man' with a 'serious goal' in mind.

The contact could have been invaluable: Roller was the chief set designer at Vienna's *Hofoper* (Court Opera House); but he was an important figure on the wider Viennese artistic scene as well.

PSYCHOANALYSING AN AGE

Each of us, said the Viennese psychologist Sigmund Freud (1856–1939), has two selves: one the conscious *ego* (the Latin for 'I'); the other an unconscious, and essentially ungovernable, *id* (the Latin for 'it'). The *id* was wholly instinctual; mere desire, unmediated by morality or even awareness. Inside each of us, Freud thought, unruly (perhaps incestuous) desires and jealous rages seethed. Uninhibitedly irrational, these furies could be spectacularly perverse: a force called *thanatos* (death drive) drove us impetuously towards our own destruction, even as our conscious reason tried to rein us back.

The subconscious was inaccessible: by definition, the patient was not conscious of it, so could not talk about it. But Freud developed a discipline through which the skilled and experienced 'psychoanalyst' could uncover its mysteries. These bubbled up to the surface in fits and starts in dreams, Freud argued – and he developed some intriguing theories about how certain symbol patterns might be interpreted. They also revealed themselves when patients were invited to talk ramblingly and randomly in the passive and undirecting presence of their analyst in a process that he called 'free association'.

Freud's therapeutic methods have remained contentious, as has much of the detailed content of his theories – do sons really at some subconscious level want to kill their fathers and sexually possess their mothers? But his basic insight – that within our thinking, reasoning minds we nurture unacknowledged, and often deeply disturbing, destructive desires – struck a chord that continues to resonate.

It certainly resonated in the wider consciousness of early-twentieth-century Vienna. Here a glittering social surface – beautiful buildings; sumptuous balls; glamorous soirées; fine art and culture – masked darker realities of poverty, squalor, crime and prostitution. Did the official Vienna, elegant and civilized, rest upon (and in crucial ways depend on the existence of) this other city in the same way the conscious *ego* rested on the unruly *id*?

Sigmund Freud had sounded the depths of the subconscious in all its cruelty – but could even he have imagined Adolf Hitler's crimes?

Hitler had high hopes of his introduction to the Brünn-born artist Alfred Roller. What happened when (indeed, if) they met remains unclear.

He had helped make history of art in 1897, when he'd joined other avant-garde artists and sculptors in breaking free from the conservative strictures imposed by the Association of Austrian Artists in what has since been known as the 'Vienna Secession'. The following year, Roller had been appointed editor-in-chief of the movement's magazine, *Ver Sacrum* ('Sacred Spring'). This journal brought together the talents of important artists such as Gustav Klimt (1862–1918), Koloman Moser (1868–1918) and Joseph Hoffmann (1870–1956) with those of writers such as the Bohemian-born Austrian poet Rainer Maria Rilke (1876–1926), German dramatist Arno Holz (1863–1929) and Belgian playwright Maurice Maeterlinck (1862–1949).

Art was no longer a separate thing, but something continuous and all-encompassing

The Secessionist style showed intriguing parallels with what the French were calling *Art Nouveau* and the Germans *Jugendstil*. The point for all these schools was not just to feature the full range of artistic endeavour but to break down the boundaries between the various disciplines, dissolving the differences between them. Although in obvious ways they'd broken with those canons that till now had conferred 'artistic' status on selected images and objects, they had done so only to elevate the importance of art still further. Art was no longer a separate thing, confined to the collection or displayed in a designated museum, but something continuous and all-encompassing. In one issue of *Ver Sacrum* (1901, IV), for example, Rilke's poem '*Vohrfrühling*'

Unencumbered by Wagner's anti-Semitic 'baggage', Anton Bruckner's music was nevertheless beloved by Hitler for its 'Germanic' grandeur.

('Early Spring') was engraved in a richly decorative design by Koloman Moser. Was this a sumptuously illustrated literary text or a stunning artwork with incorporated commentary? Which came first: the picture or the poem? Or the overall design?

I. Jahrg. Heft 1.   Einzelpreis 2 Kronen.

VER·SACRUM

ORGAN·DER
VEREINIGUNG
BILDENDER
KUENSTLER
ÖSTERREICHS·

JANUAR
·1898·

JAEHRLICH·12·HEFTE
IM·ABONNEMENT·6·FL=10M

Verlag Gerlach & Schenk, Wien, VI/1.   Alle Rechte vorbehalten.

Its cover bringing together both the visual image and the written word, *Ver Sacrum* represented a new departure for German art.

seen to have been striving for the same sort of artistic ideal: that of the *Gesamtkunstwerk* or 'total work of art'.

RALLIED OR REBUFFED?

All the indications are that the young Adolf Hitler would have jumped at the chance of joining this Modernist movement in art; that he would have embraced its aesthetic and ethnic open-mindedness, had he only been able. He certainly seems to have been eager to take up Frau Hanisch's introduction to Alfred Roller – as, surely, would any aspiring artist of this time. It wasn't just that Roller knew everyone who was anyone in the world of Viennese art: he espoused an extraordinarily open-minded and inclusive view of art itself. For a young hopeful like Hitler, he could have been an invaluable mentor; a source of advice and criticism – and of wealthy patrons. However, although he set out to visit Roller on no fewer than three occasions, Hitler's own account says nothing on what transpired.

The suspicion must be that Roller sent Hitler away with only generalized encouragement and advice, but we have no way of knowing what really happened. Some scholars have surmised that Roller urged upon his conceited would-be disciple a regime of discipline and hard work that he found distasteful when he'd been expecting a string of plum commissions. But it has also been

TOWARDS TOTALITY

Two years later, Moser and Hoffmann had gone on to found the *Wiener Werkstätte*, an art and craft collective dedicated to design in its every aspect. Art was too important to be confined to the picture frame or the pedestalled statue: they set out to surround their clients with beauty on every hand. When they remodelled an interior, they took charge not only of walls and ceilings, door surrounds and stuccoed ceiling designs but everything down through wallpaper and curtains to cutlery and cruets.

No relation to Hitler's favourite composer, the architect Otto Wagner (1841–1918) incorporated the same sort of principles into his famous designs for what he envisaged as an entirely new and artistically integrated city of Vienna. Although this wholesale revision was never to be realized, we can get an inkling of what Wagner had in mind in the stations he built for the city's underground, the *Wiener Stadtbahn*. Every inch was meticulously planned, every detail subordinated to the overall 'look'; every entrance foyer, every lamp standard; every banister of every stair.

A Koloman Moser cufflink or a Hoffmann mirror may seem a far cry from *Tannhauser* or *The Valkyries*, just as an Otto Wagner subway seems a world away from the *Siegfried Idyll*. All these different artists can, however, be

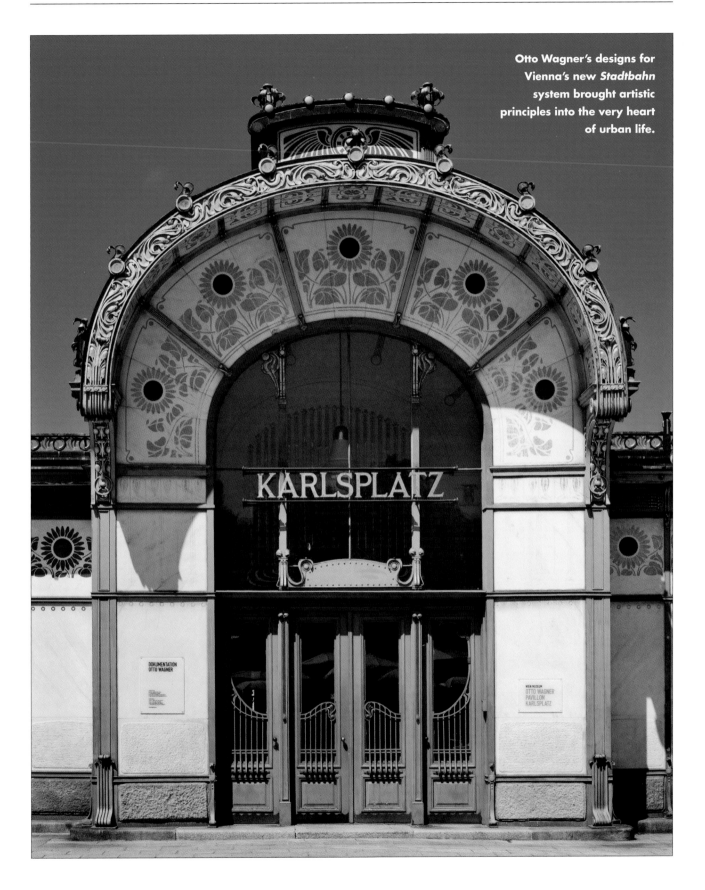

Otto Wagner's designs for Vienna's new *Stadtbahn* system brought artistic principles into the very heart of urban life.

ALL OR NOTHING

We can only guess at the residue that the idea of the *Gesamtkunstwerk* was to leave in Adolf Hitler's imagination once he had finally been forced to relinquish his ambitions as an artist or architect.

Might there be an imaginative analogy between this idea of the artistic 'total work' and the 'totalitarianism' of Hitler's vision as dictator? Nazism wasn't just an ideology: Hitler didn't just take control of the levers of power, political and economic. He wanted to imprint his personality, and the force of his vision, on every aspect of the state. From the spectacular ceremonial of the Nuremberg Rallies to the details of the uniforms of the *Schutzstaffel* (SS) and the *Hitlerjugend* (Hitler Youth), every tiny thing had to be just right.

And not just 'right', but beautiful – at least, according to a certain standard. As the Jewish Marxist thinker Walter Benjamin (1892–1940), later to be one of Adolf Hitler's victims, was to observe (in 'The Work of Art in the Age of Mechanical Reproduction', 1936), 'Fascism aestheticizes politics'.

Politics, said Goebbels, is 'the highest and most comprehensive art there is, and we who shape modern German policy feel ourselves to be artists.'

Hitler brought an artist's eye to every detail of his new society: even these *Hitlerjugend* children had to exemplify the Nazi 'look'.

suggested that Hitler was too timorous actually to make his visits. Instead, having walked up to Alfred Roller's front entrance three times, maybe he left frustrated, never having had the courage to knock at the door.

SUFFERING FOR HIS ART

Whatever happened, Hitler seems to have resolved to take his creative destiny into his own hands and to develop his artistic talent for himself. He had some savings, and dribs and drabs of income from his mother's estate, so he wasn't going to starve. He wasn't wealthy, though, by any means. The resulting poverty was no less real for being largely self-imposed. He struggled to keep up with regular rent payments and relations soured with a succession of landlords and landladies as he moved from digs to digs around the city in what was an increasingly peripatetic life.

Hitler's trajectory was spiralling slowly and steadily downwards as the weeks and months went by, his savings dwindled and his goals remained unfulfilled. Although he does seem to have sold the odd painting to passing tourists, this 'success' was double-edged. Granted, the taste such buyers had for straightforwardly realistic representations of important buildings played to the nearest thing Hitler had to an artistic strength. At the same time, the production of what amounted to

The opposite of avant-garde: some of Hitler's Vienna views were so conservative they were actually retro-set to the eighteenth century.

up-market picture postcards would not win him wider recognition, or significantly develop his skills; on the contrary, it would have reinforced the conventionality of his established style.

In the winter of 1909, Hitler seems to have sought shelter in a hostel for the homeless; the following February he moved into the Haus, a hostel in Meldemannstrasse, in Brigitennau, in the north of the city. He was to remain there for the next three

Thought to have been painted by Hitler, a couple enjoys the most innocent of Alpine idylls in this idealizing watercolour of the 1900s.

Hitler described his stay at the Haus as the 'harshest and saddest' time of his early life

years, recalled subsequently as the 'harshest and saddest' episode of his young life – though also, in more self-aggrandizing recollection, as his '*ersatz* university'.

JEWISH QUESTIONS
Even in so long and cruel a chronicle as that of European anti-Semitism, the contribution of Adolf Hitler was to stand out as uniquely

evil. It is natural, then, that historians should take an interest in the dealings he had with Jews in the years before his infamy – and that they should appreciate the ironies that these (predominantly positive) interactions now afford.

The Haus, his home for so many months, had originally been founded by a Jewish philanthropist, and Jewish charities ran the soup kitchens where Hitler was often forced to eat. But Hitler wasn't just the beneficiary of Jewish generosity: he appears to have appreciated that munificence with real warmth. Many of his fellow boarders in the Meldemannstrasse were Jews, and of these it's known

Karl Lueger (bearded, centre) stands with supporters of his Christian Social Party. He brought anti-Semitism into the mainstream as Vienna's mayor.

that a number became his friends. Some who'd known him in his Meldemannstrasse days were to register their shock at his later anti-Semitism. 'Hitler got along well with Jews,' said one: 'He once said they were an intelligent people that stuck together more than the Germans.'

In hindsight, that praise has the clear potential to turn into something more sinister; the Jews' intelligence to become 'cunning', the fact that they 'stuck together' a more menacing 'tribal' loyalty. Even so, the characterization hardly qualifies as monstrous, let alone an adequate moral or emotional

foundation for the sort of genocidal hatred Hitler was ultimately to show. For the moment, it seems, he enjoyed uncomplicated, amiable relationships with the Jews around him.

Two – Siegfried Löffner and Josef Neumann – are thought to have been his closest companions at this time. With Neumann, by trade a copper polisher but by disposition a spiritual thinker and an intellectual, Hitler is known to have had long and detailed – and seemingly sympathetic – discussions of Jewish

life and culture, and of anti-Semitism. Another Jew, the Galician immigrant Jakob Wasserberg, recalled regularly having breakfast with the future *Führer*.

So much for his social life: in so far as the young Hitler could be said to have had a 'career' in art, he also appears to have been indebted to Jewish friendship and support. Dealers like Samuel Morgenstern, Jakob Altenberg and Samuel Landsberger were the most reliable buyers for his paintings – and his favoured patrons. Hitler

Gustav Klimt was just as radical as those artists Hitler would denounce as 'degenerate': their sheer popularity let his paintings escape censure.

both literally and symbolically, elevated above the sphere of the everyday. Its frame, whether plain or ornamented, appeared to demarcate a separate and external view; to open up a 'window' on to a different, more imaginative and expressive world.

The extent of the revolution the new approach to art had wrought is clear when we consider one of Gustav Klimt's most famous works, the 'Portrait of Adele Bloch-Bauer I' (1907). Although it may present itself as a conventional painting of the traditional type, it is in no real sense a 'window' on a separate reality: instead, an artistic drama is enacted in the painted work itself.

Rather than a wealthy hostess, we seem to be watching as an alabastered face-shape emerges amid a blaze of gold. Extravagantly patterned, this effulgence is too complex and dynamic to be dismissed as a mere 'background'. The swirls of the patterns of the wallpaper behind the subject are picked up and amplified by the spiralled upholstery in which she sits enthroned – as they are in her jewelled choker and in the tumbling, yet oddly stiff, billows of her dress. There's a clear continuity here: a character of fine metalwork, marquetry or stained glass only underlined by the flatness of a painting in which perspective isn't much more than a memory. Where does this richly decorated room leave off and the richly decorated person of Mrs Bloch-Bauer begin?

Opposite: The Nazis didn't dwell on the Jewishness of Klimt's most famous subject. To them she'd simply be the 'Woman in Gold'.

found them more generous and accommodating than Christian clients, contemporaries would claim.

PORTRAIT OR PATTERN?

The scale of Modernism's achievement is apparent in every area of Vienna's post-Secession art. Arguably, and paradoxically, it is perhaps most evident in the seemingly straightforward and conventional paintings of Gustav Klimt. For centuries, the individual painting had been aesthetically iconic – as sacred to secular art as the old saints' paintings had been to the ancient churches. Displayed high up on a wall, whether in a designated art museum or in a wealthy collector's home, it occupied an exalted position,

A MONGREL MUSE

Where do Mrs Bloch-Bauer's incontrovertible beauty, style and glamour leave off and the exotic air that underpins those things begin? To be exotic is to be alien: this beauty is anything but Aryan. No Germanic blonde, but dark, and with a sinister allure, Adele Bloch-Bauer was – obviously and notoriously – Jewish. True or not, the rumour that she and Klimt had been lovers only added to her portrait's scandalous mystique; a suggestion not only of unlicensed sex but of miscegenation.

In truth, the whole Secessionist aesthetic, with its emphasis on boundary-breaking and generic commingling, could be characterized as a sort of creative *rassenschande* ('racial shame') – the pollution of artistic waters that should have been kept 'pure'. At some unspecified point, it seems, Hitler's own perspective shifted in just this way; he spurned the easy-going pluralism he'd once accepted, if not actually espoused.

How far are we to attribute this shift in attitudes in the areas both of art and of racial politics to his experiences in Vienna at this time? To put it another way, how did a young and apparently broad-minded and bohemian young man, with friends in the city's Jewish community and aspirations to join the artistic avant-garde, become the merciless persecutor of all that was racially alien or aesthetically transgressive? How far did Hitler's sense of thwarted ambition colour his approach to art and culture? How much did his humiliations at this time (not to mention the hunger and privation he endured at this stage of his 'struggle') stoke up the rage that was to drive him in his later years? And how far did former friends from the Meldemannstrasse end up being scapegoated for that sense of failure, incurring an imagined debt their fellow Jews would have to pay?

PROSTITUTION, POX AND PARANOIA

What story of a young artist's coming of age can be complete without a treatment of his heart's awakening – or more crudely, his early experiences of sex? And fair enough, given the importance such relations generally have to later psychological and emotional development. In Hitler's case, however, virtually nothing is known

Klimt's famous portrait of Adele Bloch-Bauer (1907) made a wealthy Jewish industrialist's wife into an artistic icon of the Nazi age.

EVIL-UTION

Jean-Baptiste Lamarck (1744–1829) occupies a special place in the history of science as a pioneer of the theory of evolution. Seeing the wonderful variety of nature and the way in which the different species were adapted to their different roles, he concluded that nature as we knew it was the result of a long-term process of evolution, governed by consistent scientific rules.

Key to the Lamarckian theory of evolution was the idea that acquired characteristics could be passed on. So – for example – a browsing animal that stretched its neck by repeatedly straining upwards into foliage above might over passing years end up with a slightly longer neck, which it would then pass on to its offspring. Over many generations, a giraffe-like creature might evolve. The mechanisms by which such adaptations and inheritances were to come about within the organism were a little on the sketchy side. However, Lamarck's theory did ring true intuitively, acknowledging as it did what would come to be called (in Darwinian terms) the 'fitness' of the species to their functions.

Darwin's notion of Natural Selection was to account for the evolutionary process rather better, so, in the realm of science, Lamarckian thinking was superseded. Beyond biology, however, in the area of social studies, his ideas still exercised an imaginative appeal. Whereas Social Darwinism argued for a crude idea that the finest individuals rose to the top in terms of wealth and power in our societies – to the benefit of those societies as a whole – this new-look Lamarckianism took a more pessimistic view. Just as

Lamarck would have been surprised at the uses to which his theories were adapted in the early decades of the twentieth century.

the habit of persistent reaching extended the giraffe's neck over successive generations, changing the nature of the species, so attitudes and lifestyle choices could embed themselves in human nature. Societies could 'degenerate', in short, becoming lazy and complacent, steeping themselves ever more deeply in a morass of luxury and licence. Over time, those born into such societies would 'naturally' grow morally and physically weaker, less capable of courage or of noble thought. It goes without saying that Lamarck himself would scarcely have recognized such an interpretation of his views. Nor, on the other hand, should we assume that Hitler was 'Lamarckian' in any sense. Even so, in establishing the ideas of social degeneration and of ethnic degeneracy as quasi-scientific 'facts', this philosophy significantly empowered the sort of social thinking to which young Adolf would one day be drawn.

of any romantic or sexual life during these Viennese years. That doesn't mean nothing happened, of course. Nor, for that matter, has it prevented a great deal of feverish and far-fetched speculation.

Hitler's manias and illnesses were consistent with the loneliness of leadership

One persistent theory is that at some point in 1908 Hitler had sex with a Jewish prostitute. His encounter left him with a dose of syphilis – and what must have been history's greatest grudge. There is nothing inherently improbable in the story: there is no reason why the encounter might not have taken place, nor why he might not have contracted syphilis, which was all too common a disease in Vienna at this time. Neither, though, is there any evidence for the story – only its obvious appeal as a piece of poetic justice.

For some, this has seemed to account not only for the intensity of Hitler's anti-Semitism, but the outrageously imbalanced form that anger came to take. Mental decline, including paranoid rages and mania, is a well-known symptom of syphilis in its later stages, as are other, more physical, symptoms the German dictator is believed to have had, such as encephalitis, dizziness, pustules on the neck, chest pains and accentuated heartbeat.

Of course, all these physical symptoms could stem from non-syphilitic origins; the mental ones

Darwin's idea of 'Natural Selection' transformed modern biology, but it was all too easily – and often dangerously – misunderstood.

are even easier to find an alternative explanation. Hitler's 'manias' may be consistent with late-stage syphilis, but they are also consistent with the loneliness of leadership – especially that of a state in which a cruel dictator holds sway by fear. The paranoid rages of the *Führer*'s final days may have been syphilitic in their origin, but could also have been caused by the stress you'd expect to be experienced by a war-waging dictator under final siege.

There is no doubt that, as a young man in Vienna, Hitler did associate the ideas of prostitution and of Jewishness. The sex trade was demonstrably 'controlled' by

Jews, he would insist subsequently in *Mein Kampf*. No other authority agrees with him, however (and, as elsewhere, he is far too confident in his opinion to give any supporting evidence). It does seem possible that Jewish women were overrepresented among Vienna's street prostitutes. Refugees from Russia's continuing pogroms were still streaming into the city at this time, and would have had few options in their struggle to survive. But the idea that malicious Jewish masterminds were running a trade that did so much to sap the moral energy of Austrian society surely owed more to anti-Semitic stereotype than to fact.

THE WOMAN BEHIND THE HOLOCAUST?

Is it credible, even for a second, that a single sexual encounter with a single woman could conceivably have 'caused' the criminal destruction of the concentration camps? It is hard to avoid the suspicion that the 'Jewish prostitute' story stems from an over-literal understanding of what for the young Hitler were much more general moral and symbolic fears. He would not have been the first young man to feel a misogynistic fear of female sexuality; he certainly wasn't the first German to feel deep hatred for the Jews. A few years later, in *Mein Kampf*, he was to make clear his contempt for prostitution and its prevalence in the Vienna of his day. But he seems to have viewed its existence less as an affront in its own right than as an indictment of his whole society – and the institution of bourgeois marriage at its heart. 'The cause,' he was to say in his denunciation

of twentieth-century Germany's degeneracy, 'lies primarily in our prostitution of love'.

That 'prostitution' was, it appears, more a principle than a practice, and it was to be seen most starkly not in the brothels and back alleys of Vienna but in its genteel drawing rooms. The marriage market amounted to the

'Night Conversation', Moriz Jung's picture is called – but it's who's doing all the talking, seemingly taking advantage of her oddly passive client.

NAECHTLICHES GESPRAECH

'mammonization of our mating impulse', wrote Hitler. 'Mammon' was wealth, when it was given undue importance and worshipped as a god, according to Christian scriptures. So far, so conventional a critique of bourgeois society and the institutions of marriage and family that were at its heart. Karl Marx had said something similar half a century before; the English feminist writer Mary Wollstonecraft had made the comparison between marriage and prostitution in the 1790s.

Hitler went further, however, drawing neo-Lamarckian conclusions about the effects of this situation on the German race. 'Sooner or later', he complained, this reduction of love to the level of contract and convention 'befouls our entire new generation, for instead of vigorous children of natural feeling, only the miserable specimens of financial expedience come forth.'

It made imaginative sense for the anti-Semitic mind to envisage a connection between this commercialization of love and (given the Jews' notorious covetousness) a wholesale 'Judaization' of the country's spiritual life. Morality and supposed science came together, as far as Hitler was concerned, in making cross-racial relationships not just sinful but socially destructive. 'The sin against the blood', said Hitler, 'and the degradation of the race are

Opposite: Arthur Schnitzler's works were burned by Hitler's supporters as 'Jewish filth', but revealed many of the fears in which Nazism was founded.

DEATHWISH

'Death is the side of life which is turned away from us,' wrote Rainer Maria Rilke in a letter to a friend. A constant presence, then, rather than a distant end. Not just constant but companionable, perhaps: there's a streak of melancholy running right through the German literature of the late-nineteenth and early twentieth centuries – so deep it seems to make death into a friend.

Did men and women at some level long for oblivion – extinction, even? Did they really feel Freud's 'death drive'? Was this an age that, in its deepest yearnings, hankered after its own destruction?

the hereditary sin of this world and the end of a mankind surrendering to them.'

Syphilis became emblematic of this contamination streaming through the veins of an enfeebled Germany, just as miscegenation represented 'the syphilization of our national body'.

Plagues and epidemics had been part of human life for centuries, and vague ideas of contagion were well established. What we would now call the 'germ theory' of infection was still relatively new, however. The idea of the 'virus' as a distinct type of microorganism was younger than Hitler himself. The concept of 'the Jewish virus', which now seems so repulsive, would for some in Hitler's day have had a scientific-sounding air.

SEXUAL SICKNESS

Sigmund Freud was always to insist that the poets had sensed the existence of the subconscious many centuries before he had studied and schematized it. What we would call 'Freudian' imagery – 'phallic' snakes and swords; 'vaginal' caves and landscapes that undulate like women's curves abound in the myth and literature of earlier times, as do what he called *thanatos* in all those dreams of swooning passion and descriptions of the orgasm as *petit mort* ('little death').

But sex and death were closely associated in less poetic and no less disturbing ways too. The morality of bourgeois marriage was, as many moralists, including Hitler, had appreciated, inherently hypocritical. Women were supposed to radiate chastity and childish innocence, and their husbands were expected to be 'men of substance', 'men of stature', 'men of means'. This inevitably meant that they also had to be men of a certain age and – it generally followed – 'men of the world'.

These men couldn't be expected to spend the years before they married being celibate and 'pure', which meant that an underclass of women had to live unchastely to serve their needs. This included not only the obvious group – the 'professional' sex workers, from street prostitutes to high-class courtesans – who were so noticeable a feature of early-twentieth-century Viennese society, but also the thousands of young maidservants, seamstresses and shopgirls who could be coaxed or coerced into relationships.

Those women were easily discarded when they became irksomely pressing or pregnant, but the gentleman-about-town faced other hazards that could be harder to avoid. There was no real way of knowing if a woman was as innocent as she might seem; no way of knowing in whose bed she'd been the night before.

Syphilis was not just a dangerous disease: it was the ultimate symbol of a society in which those we were closest to were ultimately unknown to us, and in which love could kill. What made the disease most powerful as a metaphor for moral evil and for social disintegration was the way its prevalence undermined the most comforting myths of middle-class respectability.

WHAT GOES AROUND...

This was the paradox around which the Austrian playwright Arthur Schnitzler (1862–1931) had constructed *Reigen* or *La Ronde* (1897), his notorious drama about the social and sexual merry-go-round of modern life.

In a series of scenes, such as 'The Prostitute and the Soldier', 'The Soldier and the Parlourmaid', 'The Parlourmaid and the Young Gentleman', 'The Young Gentleman and the Young Wife', 'The Young Wife and the Husband', he traced the contacts and connections that otherwise went unseen. In doing this he hinted at the possible transmission of syphilis – which could corrode the body and, ultimately, destroy the mind. So the sexual impulse, hard as it might be to resist, could, quite literally, drive the individual through sickness to insanity, and at the last to death.

Nor did the disease stop there: congenital syphilis was passed on to the partner and children of any such contaminated relationship, striking at the heart of the most venerated institution of the age: the bourgeois family.

Worse still, the children of such unions were born with the sickness

Schnitzler's scandalous *Reigen* (or *La Ronde*) uncovered the corruption eating away at the very heart of the bourgeois family.

at its secondary stage, working away at the central nervous system. Stunted, sickly, mentally defective or even mad, syphilitic children bore living testimony to the sins of the fathers, visited upon the next generation. Its symptoms seemed to 'act out' the process of neo-Lamarckian degeneration, in other words.

LOVE AND LOATHING

No wonder, then, that male sexual passion should so frequently have been viewed – by men themselves – as a source of anxiety and revulsion; or that the feminine beauty that sparked it should have inspired as much fear as it did love. The thought of the *vagina dentata* – the fanged vagina that bit off the male member even as it gratified its desires – seems to have haunted the male imagination of the late nineteenth and early twentieth centuries. But its significance transcends the realm of the purely sexual to encompass the anxiety of a time for which everything that seemed beautiful and enticing was at the same time terrifying; all that

---

Illnesses like syphilis were of profound importance as symbols of a sick society

---

seemed warm and welcoming was attended by feelings of fear and foreboding, while civilization was seen as the merest veneer over an abyss of horror.

This sort of anguished ambivalence appears to have been

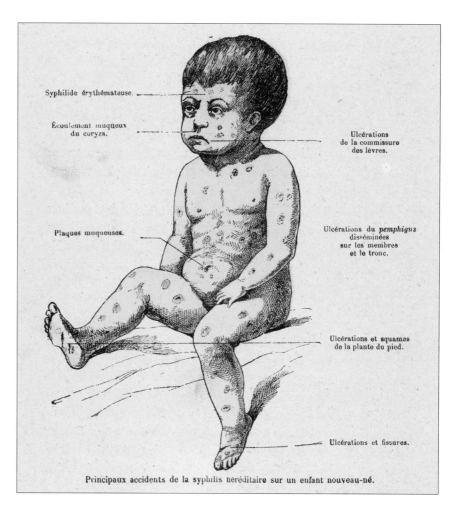

reflected throughout this culture as a whole. All that German pride was dogged by the fear of national degeneration; all that artistic endeavour seemed to be unsettling everybody; all that intellectual confidence seemed to be eroding the old certainties. As for the insights of psychology, far from offering hope of healing and happiness, it just seemed to be bringing more and more bad news.

Generally speaking, the more closely we consider the Viennese background against which Adolf Hitler was to come of age, the

Syphilis, being hereditary, hit the most innocent members of society, as this French illustration of 1883 shows.

stronger our sense of a strange and disturbing scientific-sociocultural stew of ideas, imagery and yearning. Infectious illnesses like syphilis were a reality – a cruel and destructive one – but they were also of profound importance as symbols of a 'sick' society.

That sickness was no longer just moral. Across the whole of Europe a dark and powerful sense of foreboding was forming. The continent seemed to be sinking helplessly into an ever-deepening crisis; its horizons dominated by the prospect of approaching war.

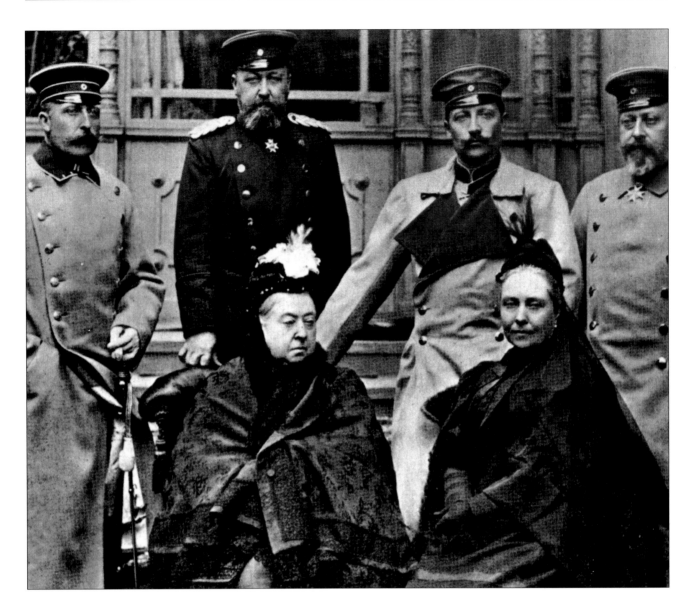

One German grandson, Alfred, Duke of Saxe-Coburg and Gotha, stands behind Queen Victoria (1894); another, Kaiser Wilhelm I, just to the right.

(commissioned in 1906). Driven by steam turbines, it was significantly faster than its predecessors. It also carried much bigger guns, enabling it to engage its enemies at a distance, beyond torpedo range. It transformed naval warfare – so much so that a whole generation

of warships was named after it. Germany commissioned its own equivalent, the *Nassau* (in 1908).

Build-ups were under way in other branches of the military too, and other European states were joining the escalating arms race. One of the worst-kept secrets of the period, the Schlieffen Plan (drawn up at Wilhelm II's orders by Count Alfred von Schlieffen in 1904, though subsequently modified) envisaged simultaneous invasions of Russia in the east and France (via

By the time war began, Hitler had left Vienna for Munich to set up as an artist there

the neutral Benelux countries) in the west. Once these possibilities had been envisaged, they couldn't be unthought: the Allied powers knew they had to be prepared.

German militarism prompted answering moves towards militarism abroad, and the top brass was brought into the heart of government. With the armed forces tail now wagging the governmental dog, war was coming to seem inevitable: the only question was exactly when.

COLONIAL COLLISIONS

There were a couple of close shaves. Berlin was increasingly alarmed at the colonial implications of Franco–British friendship. In March 1905, amid great publicity, the Kaiser paid an official visit to Tangiers, promising the Moroccan king his support against France. Paris and London alike reacted angrily to this 'First Morocco Crisis'. A second incident came six years later after Germany's deployment of the gunboat *Panther* off Agadir. The threat of war in Europe was again averted after a face-saving territorial exchange in November 1911. Germany withdrew its claims on Morocco and instead received territory in Equatorial Africa to add to its existing protectorate in Cameroon.

EUROPE EXPLODES...

The problem with such large and complex international alliances was that they produced so many potential flashpoints. The fact that Austria-Hungary was itself a large and complex international alliance hardly helped. In the end, the spark that set off the explosion came not in the colonies but in continental Europe – in Sarajevo, Bosnia.

There, in a climate of feverish activity by Slav separatists, the Serbian anarchist Gavrilo

Princip waylaid the Archduke of Austria's car, on 28 June 1914. Franz Ferdinand's assassination precipitated the 'July Crisis' and, as of 28 July, war between the Central Powers and Serbia, a Russian ally. As the Tsar's forces mobilized for war, so did France. Britain went through the form of demanding a promise from Germany that it would respect Belgian neutrality.

This was not forthcoming. Instead, the Germans put the latest revision of the Schlieffen Plan into action, invading Belgium on 4 August. What was later to become known as World War I had broken out.

Alfred von Schlieffen set the strategic course for late-nineteenth-century Germany as a determinedly expansionist military power.

... AND HITLER HIDES?

By the time war began, Adolf Hitler had left Vienna for Munich to set up as an artist there. He'd been living in the Bavarian capital since the spring of 1912. Many commentators have believed he was there specifically to avoid the Austrian draft for a war that now seemed inevitable. That was certainly the consequence of his move to Germany. Until, that is, the end of 1913, when the authorities in Munich arrested him and sent him back to face his country's conscription board. As things turned out, the problem was to

DRAFT-DODGER?

Some historians have seized on the idea that Hitler evaded his Austrian army service in order to attack his credibility as a military leader in later life; to unmask him as a coward, even. And it's true that his justification for his evasive action – his reluctance to serve an Austria-Hungary that was not a 'nation' but a collection of 'nationalities' – might seem improbably high-flown.

It's of a piece with his known opinions, though, while the 'coward' jibe can hardly be reconciled with the well-established fact that, when war broke out in August 1914, he immediately enlisted in the German army. It does appear that, for Hitler, although the defence of Austria wasn't worth giving up the artist's life, the defence of Germany was worth any sacrifice.

For now, no more than a face in the crowd – but already unmistakeable – Hitler celebrates the start of the Great War.

go away of its own accord, after Viennese officials deemed him medically unfit: he was able to go back to Munich to pick up where he had left off.

The German authorities' position is less clear: why was Hitler passed for service in Bavaria when he hadn't been in Vienna? And why was he allowed back in to Germany after his unsuccessful test in Salzburg? Despite his

Opposite: Franz Ferdinand, Archduke of Austria, was first in line to the Austro-Hungarian throne – until his assassination tipped the whole of Europe into war.

rejection by the Austrian recruiters, he had to write to ask his government's permission to serve in the German army.

'THE HARDEST OF ALL STRUGGLES'

Hitler can't be accused of having lacked the stomach for his service, even if his first fight was with the bureaucrats over all these details. In hindsight, he was to view the whole conflict in heroic, almost mythic terms, as a national struggle in which the whole of Germany

was involved. 'The struggle of the year 1914 was not forced on the masses....' he was to insist in *Mein Kampf* afterwards; 'it was desired by the whole people.'

He 'desired' it more than anyone, seemingly experiencing war's outbreak with the kind of fervour most would associate with an ecstatic excess of religious or romantic love:

'Even today I am not ashamed to say that, overpowered by stormy enthusiasm, I fell down on my knees and thanked Heaven from an

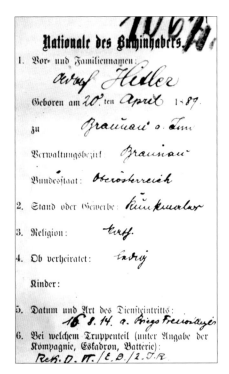

overflowing heart for granting me the good fortune of being permitted to live at this time.'

His only 'worry', he tells us, as he marched off to meet the enemy, was that he might yet miss out: 'would we not reach the front too late?'

UNDER FIRE – LITERALLY
Hitler's anxiety was to prove misplaced. As an infantryman in the 1st Company of the 16th Bavarian Reserve Regiment, *Schütze* (Private)

Hitler's military pass of 1914 offers no hint of the horrors awaiting its bearer – nor those he was later to inflict upon the world.

Hitler was to see any amount of action, starting within weeks of his arrival at the front, with the First Battle of Ypres, October 1914. Among those killed in the first day's fighting was regimental commander Colonel Julius List: the 16th Bavarian Reserve was to be known as the 'List Regiment' from that time on.

Of its 3600 men, only 611 survived the three days of the battle – an extraordinary attrition, but no more than a foretaste of things to come. One of those who did make it through was Adolf Hitler, though he was extremely lucky to, if his letter to his Munich friend Ernst Hepp is to be believed:

'We push forward four times but each time we're forced to retreat again. Of the group around me, only one's still standing – then he too falls. A shot rips off my right sleeve but – as though by a miracle – I'm still safe and sound. The fifth time we advance we manage to occupy the forest edge and adjoining farms.'

How scrupulously exact this account of events is we have no way of knowing. That Hitler handled himself more or less commendably does seem certain, though. After the battle, he was awarded an Iron Cross for rescuing a wounded comrade.

He was also promoted from the rank of private to that of lance corporal, and reassigned to duties as a *Meldeganger* or regimental runner. It's harder to be sure whether this elevation was made in recognition of his courage and resourcefulness in the field of battle or the devastation that had been wrought in the higher ranks (or both).

UNDER FIRE – FIGURATIVELY
Scholarly opinion – often, inevitably, influenced by partisan hostility or (less often) sympathy – divides on whether this was a highly dangerous role or a safe and 'soft' one behind the lines. On one side is Hitler's own account in *Mein Kampf* – a work whose

Opposite: Hitler, trying out an unusual moustache, is seen here with his comrades from the 1st Company, 16th Bavarian Reserve.

KINDERMORD

In Germany, the month-long First Battle of Ypres quickly came to be known as the *kindermord*: this was how Herod's massacre of the 'Holy Innocents' (Matthew 2, 16–18) was referred to in the German Bible.

Early accounts claimed that up to three-quarters of the 8,000 or so casualties killed on the German side had been young student volunteers. Subsequent scholarship suggests that stories of wide-eyed idealists, going singing to their deaths, were an

exaggeration. That the myth should have arisen is understandable, though. A nation entering the war on a patriotic 'high' was brought judderingly down to earth at Ypres. A certain sort of 'innocence' had assuredly been lost.

FRONTGEMEINSCHAFT

Hitler's image of the 'iron front' of a 'grey steel' helmet pushing, hard and unyielding, through the soft 'veil' of a misty past now reads as an intriguing dispatch from the age of Nietzsche and of Freud. History here is made when an essentially masculine – indeed frankly phallic – will inscribes its intention on and endows with shape and purpose an inherently feminine – passive, formless, receptive – past.

The force of the 'front' was to become central to Hitler's vision of a society built on soldierly sacrifice and directed by a strongman's will. Social thinkers since the nineteenth century had been seeking a way to build *gemeinschaft*

– a sense of community that would be warm, real and 'organic', rather than abstract and artificial in its construction. The Nazis' contribution to this (essentially Romantic) quest would be to propose the idea of a *frontgemeinschaft* – a 'front community'. Its battlefield values and virtues were to be as essential to society in times of peace as they ever had in times of war. (Not that, to their militaristic minds, the times of peace could ever be expected to last long....)

In the 1930s, the Nazi propagandist Günther Lutz was to enthuse about how a new Germany had been forged in the *dreck und*

not, the 'filth and need', of the battlefront; in the foxholes and the trenches of World War I. Its Romantic appeal apart, the idea of *frontgemeinschaft* had the obvious virtues for a militaristic society of subordinating all other experiences and expertise to those of the army. It also created a seeming sense of social solidarity that would cut clean across traditional class divides. As Hitler hints with his remark about the soldiers' fighting their way to the status of being 'sons of their nation', it established the notion (handy for him, as an Austrian incomer) that German nationality could be earned by devoted service.

Conversely, Hitler's war was Wagnerian in its grandeur. He viewed his own sufferings as the ordeal necessary to make the 'young volunteer' into an 'old soldier', and he saw that transition replicated across the army as a whole:

'It had issued old and hard from the eternal battles, and as for those who could not stand up under the storm – well, they were broken.'

The survival of the fittest under fire, in other words. A grim evolution, but its result was a 'unique army'. This was not just a formidable fighting machine, but the basis of a legend:

'Thousands of years may pass, but never will it be possible to speak of heroism without mentioning the German army and the World War. Then from the veil of the

> *Hitler viewed his own sufferings as necessary in making the 'young volunteer' into an 'old soldier'*

past the iron front of the grey steel helmet will emerge, unwavering and unflinching, an immortal monument. As long as there are Germans alive, they will remember that these men were sons of their nation.'

CAMP CAMARADERIE?
Soldiers have always tended to bond closely with their comrades. They're encouraged to: tightly ordered teamwork is essential to

the trade of war. Besides that, they can't help themselves: the loyalties and friendships forged in the field, under what would in ordinary circumstances seem unbearable stress and danger, unsurprisingly seem to have a special strength.

Fighting, obviously, is brutal: the soldier has to be prepared to kill his enemy and see his comrade die. He has to be hard; keep any empathy in check; maintain the kind of caricature 'masculinity' that defines itself by 'othering' the feminine, by keeping women (except as 'conquests') at arm's length. The sort of manly, mates-together camaraderie that tends to result is what psychologists might describe as 'homosocial'.

Does its logical conclusion lie in homosexuality? 'My dear

comrades', Hitler called them. But did his love for his brothers-in-arms go beyond soldierly solidarity? Was the ultimate male bonding to be sex? There were mutterings about Lance Corporal Hitler – first, paradoxically, because of his unease among his fellow soldiers with their abrasive banter, sexist bragging, and dirty jokes. This sort of prudishness could only mean one thing, many soldiers thought – and some scholars have agreed. Second, on account of what seems to have become an inseparable friendship with fellow courier Ernst Schmidt. The two slept side by side – Adolf 'bedded down with his whore', in the words of another comrade, Hans Mend. In his book,

The Hidden Hitler (2001), Lothar Machtan develops a detailed and in many ways persuasive case.

But the evidence, abundant as it is, is overwhelmingly circumstantial. Hitler was different – delicately nurtured, timid, a bit demure. That didn't make him gay – though of course he might have been. The only direct testimony we have come from Mend – a proven liar and would-be blackmailer.

As so often with Hitler, moreover, there's the feeling that what makes the suspicion so compelling is its appeal to our sense of poetic justice. Hitler

was to preach a message of near-parodic hyper-masculinity; homosexuals were to be sent to the death camps in his Nazi state. Yet, while it may be satisfying to think that, like many other outspoken homophobes before and since, he may have been a closet case, that doesn't make it true.

SECOND TIME AROUND
Christmas Eve! A dark night, and in a dugout deep in rural France, a group of British troops broke up a chocolate bar in celebration. The mood was relaxed. For a fleeting moment amid the stress and fear of

Signed 'A. Hitler 1917', this little sketch in pencil and watercolour depicts a ruined church on the Western Front in Flanders.

war they could sit back and rest, subside into and almost luxuriate in their exhaustion. Peace on Earth! Indeed, as nonsensical as it sounds, goodwill and friendship really seemed to reign. Across

the snow, from a foxhole just a hundred metres or so away came the sound of quietly carolling German voices: *Stille nacht…* , or, as the English knew it, 'Silent Night…'

The first Christmas of World War I has become as much a part of mythic as of military history, thanks to its spontaneous outbreak of festive fellowship and warmth. The scene above took place 30 years

Right: Adolf Hitler drew this portrait on the back of a field postcard to immortalize his friend – and maybe more – Ernst Schmidt.

later, at the final Christmas of World War II. There was to be no 'truce' this time – but the echoes of the past were inescapable. Not least because Hitler's Ardennes Offensive – as abruptly unexpected and as quixotic as it seemed – was itself the replay of a move from World War I.

In March 1918, the German army had surged westward against Amiens, striking at the vulnerable 'seam' where two great allied forces met. A last desperate throw, the Ardennes Offensive drew vital resources from a fast-crumbling Eastern Front while giving the British and Americans no more than a nasty fright. If it was ineffective, it was certainly revealing: staring defeat in the face, Hitler had gone back to his tactical roots in World War I.

A 'TRENCH PERSPECTIVE'

It has become a cliché that military commanders 'always fight the last war': old habits; old expectations; old assumptions have a way of dying hard. Was this a particular problem with Hitler's generalship? His case is complicated by the fact that he had been a fairly lowly foot soldier, not a commander, in World War I. And by the fact that, far from seeing this as a reason for humility, he appears to have felt that

Opposite: Along with postcards and pictures, the effects of a comrade (Karl Lippert) include his pass for an official trip to Lille with Private Adolf Hitler.

it gave his insights and his instincts a special weight. Rather than pulling rank over his field commanders, he pulled infantryman's experience – he'd *been there*, in all the dirt, the want and squalor.

These experiences must have given him a perspective that his field commanders – thoroughbred members of the 'officer class' – might easily be lacking in. The notorious remark by General Friedrich Fromm (1888–1945) that a civilian might have been better equipped as a commander-in-chief than a corporal in the new world war was obviously shot through with snobbishness. As we've seen, though, there's no doubt that Adolf Hitler endowed his experience in World War I with a mythic and even a mystic significance that he arguably allowed to overshadow more rational, real-world factors.

> ## Hitler endowed his experience in World War I with a mythic and even mystic significance

History conventionally associates Hitler with the idea of *blitzkrieg* – 'lightning war' – a self-consciously modern doctrine that relied on the most up-to-date technology and the strength, speed and mobility these brought. The Battle of France and (at least in its opening stages) Operation 'Barbarossa' offered textbook examples of this philosophy in action. However, Hitler's generals were frequently to complain of their *Führer*'s 'trench perspective'.

However radical his rhetoric of *blitzkrieg*, in all its dash and daring, his instincts seem to have been for a more static style of warfare. Standing firm and slugging it out: that was how the hero fought. This was what Hitler's men were to do at Stalingrad, long after their commanders felt this was strategically justified.

This, Hitler believed, was where his character – and that of a new Germany – were forged: in the tumult of the trenches of the Great War.

ALL AT SEA

Hitler's account of Germany's collapse in 1918 is memorable both in its obvious anger and in its vividness. But it is also intriguing in more nuanced ways. One curious detail is the blame attributed to naval sailors, who are lumped together with Jewish agitators in his complaint.

'Sailors arrived in trucks', wrote Hitler, 'and proclaimed the revolution; a few Jewish youths were the "leaders" in this struggle for the "freedom, beauty, and dignity" of our national existence. None of them had been at the front.'

There was a literal basis to Hitler's hostility to the seamen. They weren't – and never had been – bound by the same code as his beloved soldiers. Teamworkers under quasi-industrial conditions, seafarers had been comparatively quick to unionize in civilian life, to make 'mutinous' cause together in military navies. The action of the crew of Russia's *Potemkin* (1905) was to be an inspiration to the Russian Revolution; 1931 was to see a serious revolt in Britain's Royal Navy at Invergordon. And, as Hitler's account suggests, a revolt of sailors (at the naval port of Wilhelmshaven, Lower Saxony) was to precipitate the proclamation of a German Republic in October 1918.

For Hitler, however, historical fact seems to have chimed neatly with his own symbolic scheme in barring these seaborne fighters from his sacred *frontgemeinschaft*. This community, it appears, was open only to those who had fought on the literal land front; seafarers' service and sacrifice had not signified.

As his country's supreme commander, his grudging way with the Navy was frequently to be remarked upon – and may well have been disastrous. Did it all come down to so deep a prejudice?

Breaking out before the war was over, the Wilhelmshaven Mutiny was seen by Hitler as showing the unpatriotic character of Germany's seamen.

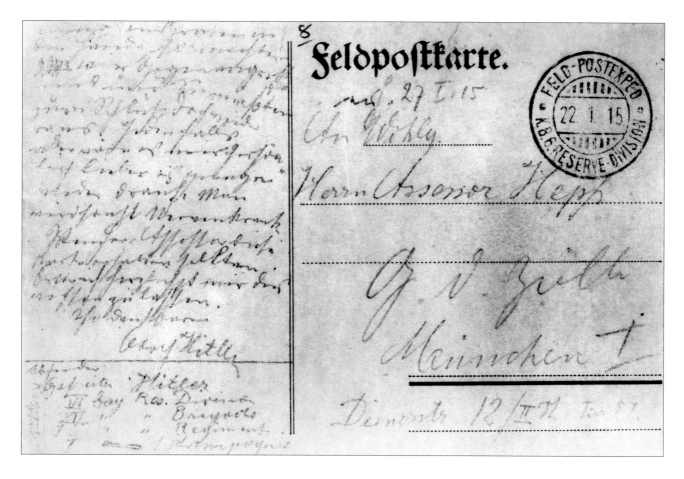

Adolf Hitler sent this postcard to his fellow-runner Karl Lanzhammer at the front whilst he himself was recuperating behind the lines.

back as spirits of vengeance to the homeland which had cheated them with such mockery of the highest sacrifice which a man can make to his people in this world? Had they died for this, the soldiers of August and September 1914?...'

Again, the talk is all of blood and earth – as far as Hitler's mythic characterization of what had happened went, the recent conflict had been exclusively a land war.

And what is all this about 'the soldiers of August and September 1914'? What of those who joined up or were drafted in the months and years that followed? Again, as with his country's naval seamen, Hitler seems concerned to narrow down the available array of

German heroes. Without explicitly doing down those conscripted later, Hitler clearly felt he was a founder member of this band of brothers. And he repeatedly singles out the contribution of the 'old soldiers' (like himself) for special praise. Neither does he shrink from saying that those who enlisted in the final stages of the war were 'mostly worthless', 'not a reinforcement but a weakening of our fighting strength'.

It seems unlikely that Hitler really wished to disparage or dismiss the contribution of those who joined up later: it's just that he was more interested in building up

the semi-mythic significance of the old soldiers' sacrifice. He does find space to sympathize with the plight of the 'German mother' – another mythic archetype:

'Was this the meaning of the sacrifice the German mother made to the Fatherland when with sore heart she let her best-loved boys off, never to see them again? Did all this happen only so that a gang of wretched criminals could lay hands on the Fatherland?'

Ultimately, the importance of World War I for Hitler, inestimable as it was, lay not in its historical implications but in its mythic power.

CHAPTER 4

POLITICAL BEGINNINGS

In historic hindsight, Hitler's rise to power can easily seem inevitable: it would certainly have been harder for him to hijack a more successful, stable post-War Germany. At every stage of his ascent, however, he had to call on all his ruthless cunning. And his genuine genius as a public speaker.

Stabbed in the back. There was no other way Hitler's heroes could have been defeated but by those their country had nurtured as its own. Disenchanted nationalists in their thousands shared this view: that Germany could simply have lost the war was unthinkable. Notwithstanding the difficulties and costs of waging a four-year conflict on two extensive fronts, with the world's wealthiest industrial powers ranged to the west and the Russian Empire to the east, Germany's invincibility was taken as read. For the Fatherland to have fallen, there must have been a parricide.

Opposite: Hitler cuts a commanding figure against the rail of a Baltic steamer in this photograph from 1921.

What became known as the *Dolchstoßlegende* – the 'stab-in-the-back' myth – was to take a strong hold on the conservative consciousness in the post-war period. Somewhere along the line, the idea became associated with the story of the legendary hero Siegfried, so famously revived by Richard Wagner in his *Der Ring des Nibelungen*. Just as the Greek hero Achilles had his heel, Siegfried's invulnerable skin can only be pierced in one tiny spot at the centre of his back; it's there that, in *Götterdämmerung* ('Twilight of the Gods') he is treacherously run through by his assassin.

Jews and communists had come together, an insidious, unscrupulous and cunning enemy within. Cosmopolitan by nature, outsiders by tradition, Germany's Jews despised the idea of a nationhood against which Marxist thinking took ideological exception. The workers' state would be international, Karl Marx (1818–83) – a Jew himself, of course – had insisted. To his followers, the recent hostilities had been a capitalists' quarrel. 'A bayonet is a weapon with a worker at both ends,' Lenin had supposedly said. What did it matter to the masses who 'won' the war? For such people, national adversity had been no more than an opportunity. Trade unionists had done their worst to weaken the war economy. Now they'd got their way: Germany was a leftist-dominated, Jew-ridden republic – and (perhaps the same thing) a defeated, shattered state.

THE SPIRIT OF WEIMAR
On paper, things looked good – to the less fanatical outside observer,

at any rate. The defeat of Wilhelm's warmongering Reich was a victory for civilization and democracy. The elections of 19 January 1919 were the freest ever. Not just men of all classes but women got to vote. While the Socialist Party secured the largest poll, it didn't win well enough to form a government, so it had to form a coalition with the liberal Progressives and the *Zentrum* or Centre Party. Guaranteed moderation, in other words: it augured well.

Weimar was safely removed from the political ferment of Berlin

The new national assembly convened in Weimar on 6 February 1919. Goethe's hometown had been chosen as the capital of the new German Republic with good reason. With its picturesque architecture and its literary associations, it stood as a reminder of what German civilization had achieved in an earlier, more peaceful age, before the lust for military power had brought it down. It also had the advantage of being safely removed from the violent ferment of Berlin. The National Assembly needed to be able to get on with its work without distractions. There was a constitution to be determined, a president to be appointed, a

The German elections of 1919 were the freest ever, but the euphoria was short-lived. Soon the country would be plunged into economic crisis.

government formed and a peace treaty agreed upon with the victorious powers.

Another way of seeing Weimar's remoteness, though, was as irrelevance; its well-meaning decency looked like weakness, its coalition government like constant compromise. It wasn't delivering the goods economically, either: the iconic image of the commuter carrying his wages home in a wheelbarrow may be exaggerated, but the hyperinflation of 1921–4 was no mere myth. A sense of rolling crisis was taking hold.

POST-TRAUMATIC
Germany's soldiers were especially hard hit. Hitler's former comrades were at best bewildered and confused. Many had terrible injuries, or suffered from 'shell shock' (PTSD, as it would now be called). Even the most fortunate faced problems picking up their former lives. The specific psychological problems of the returning veteran have long been recognized. After life in the war zone, peacetime life can be paradoxically hard to bear. The suffering may have stopped; the fear of death at any moment may have been banished; but a deep and seemingly irremovable residue of stress remains. On the front, at least, the suffering soldier can look to his comrades for support; back home, no one appears to understand.

There are, moreover, ways in which life on the front can be more comfortable: life is directed; every minute managed; every soldier has his place. Returning veterans have posed problems for society after

February 1919 saw the opening of the Weimar Assembly. It all went fairly rapidly downhill from there.

every major conflict since ancient times. Only recently, however, have the depth and complexity of their psychological difficulties been recognized.

Many of these difficulties must have been faced by Hitler, back in Munich; his occupation of four years gone; no home; no job; no obvious direction to pursue. We have no basis for claiming that he suffered PTSD – or any other

mental health condition. The evidence on which such a diagnosis could be based does not exist. He was rootless, though; marooned in Munich, without work or relations in the city and with no obvious direction to pursue.

Allied to the affliction in his eyes, moreover, the sense of disappointment and disgust he felt at his country's capitulation seems to have brought him to the brink of breakdown. In that regard, it doesn't seem so far-fetched to see his plight (as he does himself) as mirroring Germany's; as narrator of

Mein Kampf, he becomes a sort of symbolic 'Every German'.

Like his country, Hitler was crushed, defeated; deeply frustrated by his sense that, just when it seemed most vital that he set about rebuilding a life in ruins, there was so little clarity about what direction he should take.

'Endless plans chased each other through my head. For days, I wondered what could be done, but the end of every meditation was the sober realisation that I, nameless as I was, did not possess the least basis for any useful action.'

THE SECRET AGENT

In the end, Hitler was to find his scope for action by sitting still. A soldier he'd become, and so a soldier he'd remain. Having re-enlisted in the army, by July 1919 Hitler was being assigned to intelligence work as an agent of the *Aufklärungskommando* (Reconnaissance Commando). His specific task was the infiltration of the German Workers' Party (DAP), a small and still scarcely significant group that had been founded just a few months before. It was the creation of Anton Drexler (1884– 1982). A native of Munich, where DAP activities were for the most part focused, he had worked as a toolmaker and as a locksmith. He had literary interests too, however, and wrote poetry, but had made the main business of his life the struggle to promote the German nation and denounce the depredations of the Jews. He had an able and eloquent supporter in the journalist Karl Harrer (1890–1926).

Hitler, as we've seen, was already thinking along comparable lines: to join the DAP and befriend its leaders was not just a duty but a pleasure. As a soldier, he was to say, he brought a new can-do spirit to the party: 'I ... had forgotten how to say: "that's impossible", or "it won't work"; "we can't risk that'; "that is too dangerous," etc.,' allowing DAP members to 'think bigger' than they had before. He, for his part, was discovering new talents he hadn't realized he possessed: 'I could speak!', he realized on addressing his 'electrified' first meeting.

His responsibility to report back to his superiors in army intelligence appears quite quickly to have slipped his mind – though at exactly

EXPRESSIONIST EXCESSES?

The loss of Adolf Hitler apparently unnoticed, German artistic life went on – though it now took death, destruction and social disintegration as its themes. 'There has been enough dying! Let no more fall...' cried Käthe Kollwitz (1867–1945) after the loss of her young son Peter in the war. She was to sculpt a monument in stone to him – and to his lost comrades. She made her mourning the main subject of her anguished art.

Inspired by her example, a new generation of German Expressionist artists set out to capture what they saw. For men like Max Beckmann (1884–1950) and George Grosz (1893–1959), however, only the techniques of what had once been caricature could do justice to the society they saw. 'My drawings expressed my despair, hate and disillusionment,' Grosz was to recall. The legacy of the Great War,

all around him, was just waiting to be sketched:

'I drew soldiers without noses; war cripples with crustacean-like steel arms; two medical soldiers putting a violent infantryman into a strait-jacket made of a horse blanket ... I drew a skeleton dressed as a recruit being examined for military duty.'

The maimed and mutilated veterans we see in the street scenes of Otto Dix (1891–1969) symbolized the dismemberment of a whole society. Hitler was eventually to denounce most of this art as evil and

Käthe Kollwitz's 'Mother with her Dead Son' captured the anguish of a nation.

'degenerate', but its critique of Weimar society was not unlike his own.

what point this happened remains unclear. Quite what benefit the authorities had ever derived from their agent in the DAP it's hard to know: spying is, by definition, a secretive and murky business.

There's no doubt that Hitler threw himself into his new role with enthusiasm: he was soon embroiled in the internal politics of a party approaching a parting of the ways. While admiring Karl Harrer's intellect, Hitler was impatient with his esoteric elitism – he seemed more interested in running a secret society than a real mass party. Allying himself with Drexler and his friend Dietrich Eckart (1868–1923),

Hitler worked hard towards the expansion of what would soon be renamed the National Socialist German Workers' Party (NSDAP). Hitler drew on his designer's talents to create the party's banner: a black swastika on a white circle with a bright red background.

SMALL BEGINNINGS, GREAT EXPECTATIONS

With its membership of only 60, the NSDAP was barely a party at all; it was far from being the mass movement Hitler dreamed of. Even after opening the party roll at number 500, to give an inflated sense of its size, he struggled to add members for some time. He, Hess and Rosenberg were there from the start, as was Hans Frank (1900–46), who was later to be his lawyer and to preside over the judiciary in occupied Poland.

The breakthrough came in February 1919, when Hitler addressed what they had worked hard to make the biggest meeting yet. 'At 7.15', Hitler was to recall, 'I entered the Festsaal of the Hofbräuhaus on the Platzl:

'My heart nearly burst for joy. The gigantic hall – for at that time it still seemed to me gigantic – was overcrowded with people, shoulder to shoulder, a mass numbering almost 2,000 people.'

Many, of course, were communists, come to disrupt proceedings – which indeed they did. To Hitler's excitement, however, the longer he spoke, the

Anton Drexler, anti-Semitic visionary, had founded the DAP, but he lacked the political skills to resist the rise of Hitler.

more emboldened and encouraged his supporters grew and soon their cheers were drowning out the Leftists' catcalls; the communist thugs were being seen off by Nazi converts. By the end of the evening, Hitler knew, he said, that 'the principles of a movement which could no longer be forgotten were moving out among the German people'. (Karl Harrer could see it too, it seemed: he chose that night to tender his resignation, realizing that 'his' small and secret German Workers' Party was no more.) For Hitler, it was the moment of truth:

'A fire was kindled from whose flame one day the sword must come which would regain freedom for the Germanic Siegfried and life for the German nation.'

The 'stab-in-the-back' of 1918 would be undone.

PROPAGANDA AND THE PEOPLE

Hitler considered the Hofbräuhaus meeting supremely significant when he wrote up this little bit of history

Above: Polished and statesmanlike: Hitler looks every inch the politician in this photo from 1921, but he was quickly to discard this 'softer' image.

Right: Hitler's DAP card from 1920 lists him as member number 555, but he wasn't going to stop till he was uncontested number 1.

Dating from 1919, the first known shots of Hitler on film appear to show him heading a demonstration of the DAP.

in *Mein Kampf*. No one else at the time seems to have done so: it went more or less unnoticed in the Munich press. But Hitler didn't deal in facts; more at home in a realm of myth and sub-Wagnerian fantasy, he surmised that the overwhelming mass of his fellow Germans felt much the same. Even so, he set himself above them as one destined to lead, and to be followed by his people. He made no attempt to conceal this disdain for democracy, even in so public a testament as *Mein Kampf*. 'The receptivity of the great masses is very limited, their intelligence is small, but their power of forgetting is enormous.'

An unappealing view, perhaps, in one who hoped to lead his people, but absolutely essential to who Hitler was. He had low cunning, dark charisma, eloquence and ruthlessness in spades, but these can't explain the extraordinary scale of his ambition or the extent of his eventual rise. The nearest he came to genius in his make-up, arguably, was his deep and seemingly

instinctual appreciation of the importance of propaganda – and his consummate understanding of how it worked. Hence his indignation at the kind of propaganda Germany had issued during the war. It had been too moderate; too nuanced; too scrupulously prepared to acknowledge faults and grievances on both sides, he claimed. By contrast, British and French propaganda had maintained a steady stream of mendacious stories of 'Hunnish' atrocities on the one hand and acts of Allied heroism on the other.

The ineffectiveness of this propaganda effort had been

OCCULTIST OPTIONS

Anton Drexler and Karl Harrer formed a bridge between 'street' versions of Far Right politics, like the DAP, with the much more rarefied world represented by the Thule Society. Named for the mythic northern country of classical Greek legend, this circle celebrated Germany's Nordic, Aryan past – which its members believed had originated on this landmass, long since lost.

Conventional ethnologists had for a long time argued (with good reason) that the real-life Aryans had come from the steppes of Central and Western Asia. For a new generation of German mystics, though, such 'Oriental' origins could not be accepted: they developed elaborate theories to demonstrate how the north European nations were the descendants of an ancient race called the Hyperborea – their name a reference to their origins on the 'Far Side of the North Wind'.

As absurd as it may now seem, such speculation was highly popular in the post-war period – and not just in Germany. Neither was it confined to the uneducated: devotees included writers such as Arthur Rimbaud (1854–91) and William Butler Yeats (1865–1939). The sense that civilization was going down the drain was leading

many thinking people to explore possible alternative or occult realities; the mass bereavement of the war had helped foster a craze for clairvoyancy and spiritualism, with their promise of real contact with the dead. Several future Nazi

luminaries such as Rudolf Hess (1894–1987) and Alfred Rosenberg (1893–1946) were active members of the Thule Society, while others attended or addressed the circle's meetings. That said, there is no evidence that Hitler ever did.

Centring on the swastika, the emblem of the Thule Society suggests a movement poised uneasily between mystic philosophy and violence.

'Best wishes from the Hofbräuhaus',
reads this postcard from Adolf Hitler,
from the scene of one of his most
important early triumphs.

VINDICTIVE VERSAILLES

The impact of Germany's defeat
on popular morale was obviously
shattering, especially given all the
sufferings that had gone before. But
people are on the whole resilient
and quick to look to the future and
put the past behind them, rather
than to dwell on disasters that had
gone before.

For the victorious Allies, though,
this sort of recovery was not to
be sanctioned. Why should the
great aggressor (as they saw it) go
unpunished? Germany was in the
doghouse internationally, and there
it must remain. Those negotiating

not just an administrative but a
massive *moral* failure, Hitler felt;
another great betrayal by those
who should have been in charge.
What made Hitler's dictatorship
so powerful was to be his mastery
of the media of communication
and the skill with which he made
himself the 'narrator' of everything
that went on.

GENDERED AGENDAS

Democracy is always limited: we
can't ask everyone about every
single decision. Government of the
people, by the people, for the people
can realistically only go so far.
When we speak of the democratic
'will', therefore, we're talking
loosely – metaphorically, even.
Modern democracies muddle along,
making the best compromise they
can between consultation and the
practical need to keep things going
and get things done.

But for extremists, both of Left
and Right, the fact that democracy
has necessarily been limited has
been seen as proof that it is no more
than a pious lie. Lenin's contempt
for liberalism and its vaunted

freedoms is well known: what
mattered was not the bourgeois
individual but the working class.
For Hitler, by contrast, the crucial
thing was Germany *über alles*
('above all else'): the country's
citizens existed to serve the state.

It's here that we see one of the
distinctions between the anti-
democratic elitism of the Left
and the anti-democratic elitism
espoused by Hitler and the Right.
Both claimed to have mobilized
the political power of the 'People'.
For the Left, however, the mass of
workers was seen as masculine;
a source of brute but undirected
strength that had to be harnessed
and guided by the leadership.

(Hence all those well-muscled,
clenched-fist salutes on the party's
posters.)

For Hitler, by contrast, the
People 'are so feminine by nature
and attitude that sober reasoning
determines their thoughts and
actions far less than emotion and
feeling.' Like the wife or daughter
in a family, they had to be guided,
directed by a higher masculine will:
this was ultimately to be embodied
in himself as *Führer*. In hindsight,
such an opportunistic marriage
of sub-Nietszchean 'Superman'
philosophy and old-fashioned family
values seems quite laughable, but it
spoke with thrilling immediacy to
Hitler and his henchmen.

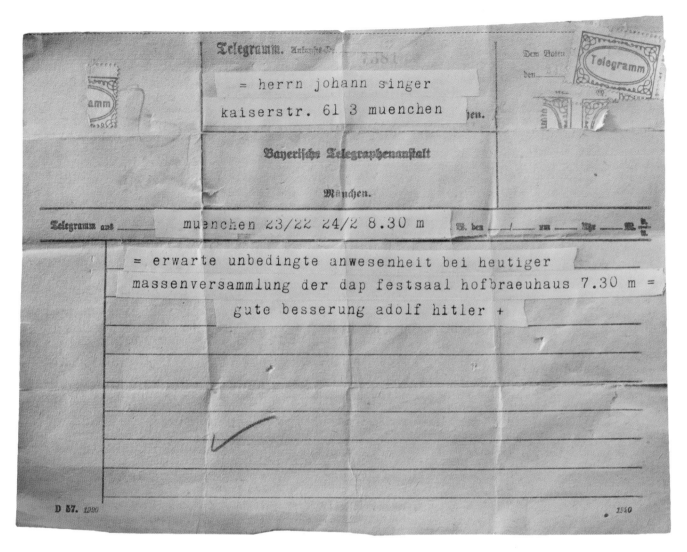

A telegram sent by Hitler to fellow-DAP activist Johann Singer fine-tunes arrangements for a mass meeting at the Hofbräuhaus.

the terms of the new peace, at Versailles, outside Paris, were resolved on this.

The punitive intentions of the final settlement, sealed by a treaty of 28 June 1919, were only too apparent. Not only would Germany have to disarm and give up territories to its wartime enemies: it would have to make reparations to them, to the tune of 130-odd billion Marks. It has been suggested that the harshness of Germany's treatment was the result of disagreement among the Allied powers. Some on the French side (perhaps understandably) wanted

to see Germany left as so much scorched earth; others argued for a more forgiving line.

This, they argued, was dictated as much by pragmatism as by moral magnanimity: there had to be, first, a real chance for Germany to rejoin the community of nations; second, some meaningful incentive for it to keep the peace and strive. As things were, no matter how hard Germans worked to rebuild their country, they could never hope to see their circumstances improve.

No matter how resolutely they pushed forward, they would be standing still, held back by their never-ending reparations debt. Why work? Why invest? Why build for a future it seemed would never come? Germany was thoroughly mired in economic gloom.

TAKEN TO EXTREMES

The Versailles Treaty, it is generally agreed, was a disaster for Germany – and ultimately, of course, for Europe as a whole. More damaging even than the economic impact of the reparations burden on Germany, though, was the discredit it brought on constitutional politics in the country. Those parties that sought to keep the rules and steer a moderate, conciliatory course were able to offer only more of the same – poverty and pain. Those decent, moderate assembly members who did their best to help their country meet its obligations under impossible conditions were derided as 'fulfilment politicians' – i.e., pets of the foreign powers.

> *Impatient for improvement, people listened eagerly to the quick-fix solutions of the Left and Right*

Impatient for improvement, despairing of the promises of the respectable parties of benefits on the far-off political horizon, people listened eagerly to the quick-fix solutions of the Left and Right. Smash capitalism, said the socialists, and the agony would be at an end; rise up against the liberal establishment and the foreign oppressors, urged the Nazis.

ANTI-SEMITIC OVERTURES

Of course, Jews were also characterized as part of the problem; as an overarching and

Amidst the splendour of France's *ancien régime*, peace in Europe was effectively consigned to the past. The Versailles Treaty made further conflict inevitable.

sinister presence in German life. Anti-Semitism was by no means new: it had a European history that went back to medieval times. Nor, in the light of the 'Final Solution' that was to come, does it seem especially surprising to find it associated with Hitler here. But it does appear to have been a new development. We should not perhaps exaggerate the importance of the friendships he is supposed to have had with Jews during the Vienna years; these could have co-existed with the sort of prejudice that was often the norm in Central European society at the time. Even so, there is no evidence to suggest that Jew hatred lay at the heart of Hitler's political thinking in quite the way it was beginning to do now.

In Hitler's rhetoric of the early 1920s, an ancient scapegoat was reinvented, an age-old stereotype retouched to take account of recent developments in race theory, and of those in the ideological and economic spheres. The Jew, for Hitler and his Nazis, was the living embodiment of cosmopolitanism – as ruthlessly acquisitive as he was rootless. To some extent, the one trait begat the other: his lack of any homeland left him without local loyalties, or any conscience as far as the exploitation as his host country was concerned. He grasped and gouged without the slightest pity and with all his might.

That instinctive internationalism that had been bred into him by

Opposite: Members of the public smirk with complicity as a Jewish man is harassed by police in the early 1920s. Anti-Semitism was already on the rise.

FROM CABARET TO BEER HALL

For many of us, Weimar Germany comes most excitingly alive in all its decadence and daring in the works of English writer Christopher Isherwood (1904–86) or in the Broadway show *Cabaret* (1966; a movie followed in 1972), based loosely on his work. Typically owned and run by Jews, their performers openly flouted respectable race- and sex-taboos and made irreverent fun of society's most sacred norms to the delight of a self-consciously sophisticated clientele. Honest, law-abiding citizens naturally shunned such places: for them there were ordinary pubs – and, increasingly, big brewery-run 'beer halls'. Very different from the traditional tavern, with its crowded bar and its pokey little nooks and niches, these were huge halls were thousands could come together to drink, joke and sing.

hundreds of generations of exile allowed him effortlessly to span the contradictions between the modern world's two great evils. Despite their differences, capitalism and communism shared an indifference to nations and to the life and welfare of the 'little man': they belonged together in Hitler's lexicon of hate. And both were under the control of the Jews – those who ran the banks and finance houses and those who ran the Bolshevik Revolution in Russia, which was even now threatening the peace of the whole world. The Jews were 'undermining' Germany, said Hitler; they had to be 'removed' from society; already, he was calling for them to be arrested and interned.

Hitler was also already expressing his anti-Semitism in ominously genocidal-sounding terms. 'You don't,' he insisted, talk about the finer points of handling parasites and bacilli. 'They're simply eradicated, as quickly and thoroughly as possible.' The Jew was a toxic presence among the people, he complained; a 'racial tuberculosis' that had to be 'removed'.

TAKING A LEAD

A froth of angry patriotism; a generous apportioning of blame to namby-pamby politicians; a dash of anti-communism; copious quantities of anti-Semitic bile. Hitler's rhetoric was prepared to a repellent recipe but it went down well at the beer-hall meetings he addressed. As the weeks and months went by, he was becoming a well-recognized figure on the Far Right scene – and an essential asset to the NSDAP. As yet, though, it all seemed oddly undirected: Hitler was whipping up excitement and emotion to no obvious final end. He may have been telling the truth when, repeatedly, he denied any higher personal ambition at this time than to be the 'drummer' whose hypnotic beat would get his countrymen on the march.

'THE GREAT MAN SOUTH OF THE ALPS'

Italy's role in the Great War had been complicated. A member of the 'Central Powers' grouping with Germany, Austria-Hungary, and Ottoman Turkey, it had disagreed with their decision to go to war. In the spring of 1915, indeed, it had entered the conflict on the Allied side and so had ultimately emerged among the victors. It didn't feel like a winner, though: its economy exhausted, Italy had struggled to see any sign of a reward. The more so after the Versailles Conference had slighted its territorial demands.

Political polarization was inevitable: there was industrial and agrarian unrest; reaction among the urban middle class and the rural landowners; and a liberal government under siege on either side. A journalist and former socialist who had served jail time for his criticisms of Italy's involvement in the recent 'imperialist' war, Benito Mussolini (1883–1945) had fallen out with his former comrades on the Left. The Fascist Party he founded in 1919 took its name from the *fasces* (the bundle of rods tied together with the axe that could be used to cut them) carried as an emblem of authority by the *aediles* who had kept order in ancient Rome.

The whole appeal of fascism was its authoritarianism, and Mussolini's personal dominance as *Il Duce* ('The Leader') was essential to its message. It wasn't just explicitly but *aesthetically* authoritarian – or so it seemed as its black-shirted young male supporters strutted in village squares and city streets. It all got much more serious when, on the evening of 27 October 1922, tens of thousands of these *Camicie Nere* ('Blackshirts') converged on the country's capital. When the government appealed to Victor Emmanuel III to call a state of emergency, the king flatly refused. The door was open for Mussolini to establish Europe's first fascist dictatorship – and set the political target at which Hitler would aim.

Mussolini's March on Rome showed Hitler how a show of strength could bring real power.

Hitler and supporters stand at a wreathed war monument, around 1920: the Nazis co-opted the courage of the heroes of the past.

In the summer of 1921, however, party dissidents took advantage of Hitler's absence in Berlin with Dietrich Eckart to try to forge a merger with the German Socialist Party (DSP – despite its name another Far Right group). We have no way of knowing whether this had always been his plan or was just his spur-of-the-moment reaction to dramatic new developments, but Hitler took advantage of the crisis to seize power. Threatening Drexler with his resignation if he didn't yield him the leadership, he left the original founder of the DAP with no real choice. So central had Hitler made himself to the fortunes of his party that it had become inconceivable to let him go.

In full charge now, Hitler began to give rein to his wider fantasies of power, looking to Italy, where Benito Mussolini was cutting such a swathe. He was full of admiration at *Il Duce*'s 'March on Rome'. 'How miserable and dwarfish,' he observed, 'our German would-be statesmen seem by comparison, and how one gags with disgust when these nonentities, with boorish arrogance, dare to criticise this man who is a thousand times greater than they; and how painful it is to think that this is happening in a land which barely half a century ago could call Bismarck its leader.'

Hitler stands flanked by a couple of his Brownshirts in 1923. By now he was beginning to wield real power.

POLITICS AS PERFORMANCE

Mussolini's March on Rome had been no ordinary coup. The Blackshirts hadn't actually seized power themselves. What they had put on in Italy's capital had been no more than a show of strength. At the same time, however, it had showed that, when it comes to politics, the perception of strength is what really counts. Hitler had already taken a leaf out of *Il Duce*'s book in coming up with a paramilitary 'look' for his paramilitary *Sturmabteilung* (SA).

Uniformed yobs indispensable for roughing up Jews and for defending Nazi meetings against Leftist foes, these 'stormtroopers' were *Camicie Nere* in all but shirt colour – they wore brown.

While this paramilitary fashion must have played well to the macho fantasies of Hitler's young male followers, it appealed to many ordinary civilians as well. The apparent impotence of parliamentary politics and the paralysis of an economy hit by constant strikes fostered a

yearning for a politics that would act decisively to 'get things done'. Perhaps paradoxically, the army was the one institution never blamed for Germany's defeat in the war. Many looked to militarism to lead their country out of chaos. To be sure, the SA weren't real soldiers. Again, though, it was the perception that mattered most. Mussolini had shown that a skilfully managed stunt could help

Opposite: Strikes in 1922, whilst apparently a show of left-wing strength, gave Hitler and his Brownshirts an opportunity to build influence.

Opposite: Ludendorff's support for Hitler came as a surprise to many Germans, but he shared the Nazis' feeling that their nation had been betrayed.

secure real political power. Hitler resolved that he would do the same.

GRIM REALITIES

It is hardly surprising that this sort of theatrics should have appealed: there was nothing remotely reassuring about the realities of German life just now. By the end of 1922, the futility of 'fulfilment' politics was becoming clear. In December, Germany defaulted on the deliveries of wood and coal it was due to make to France and Belgium. Those two neighbours registered their annoyance by sending their troops into the Ruhr. Ignominious indeed – and when the Weimar government promptly called on the population of this great mining and industrial region to offer passive resistance the response was spectacular: the resulting strikes went on for weeks, then months.

Any sense of satisfaction was short-lived, however. As 1923 went on it became clearer by the month just how dearly Germany was paying for this expression of patriotic pride. By September, the struggle was costing 40 million gold marks a day in benefits. In printing ever more money to pay strikers for being unproductive, the Republic

MUNICH PUTZI

One of Hitler's closest friends at this time was the young German-American publisher Ernst Hanfstaengl (1887–1975). 'Putzi', as he was popularly known, had been born and brought up in Munich. In adolescence, however, he had spent some years in his mother's native United States; he had been to Harvard, from where he'd graduated in 1909.

Placed in charge of the New York office in his father's publishing house, he got to know such luminaries as then-senator Franklin D. Roosevelt (1882–1945) and the writer and bohemian Djuna Barnes (1892–1982), to whom he became engaged. Angered by anti-German feeling in America, however, he broke it off to return home after the war.

Even so, he had American friends: it was to help out a diplomat of his acquaintance, indeed, that in 1922 he went to hear Hitler speak. An instant convert, he

For several years, German-American Ernst Hanfstaengl was close to Hitler – and an important link to the wider political world.

quickly became the future dictator's friend. As the Nazis rose to power, however, he made an enemy of Joseph Goebbels (1897–1945). Finally, believing he was the object of an assassination plot, he fled. Arrested by the British, he spent the World War II years interned before being released and repatriated to Germany.

was fuelling hyperinflation. A loaf of bread cost 200,000,000,000 marks.

THE MUNICH *PUTSCH*

It was against this background that Hitler began planning what has gone down in history as the 'Beer Hall *putsch*'. (A *putsch*, in German, is what in English is called a 'coup'.) His mounting ambition and his persuasive powers were both to be underlined by his success in recruiting the distinguished General Erich von Ludendorff (1865–1937) to this conspiracy. Ludendorff was

known for his fiercely nationalistic espousal of the 'stab-in-the-back' theory of German defeat, so, from an ideological point of view, his participation was not surprising. He was a nationally famous figure, though, and one who was generally respected for his integrity. Securing his support had been a major achievement.

Neither Hitler nor von Ludendorff were especially unusual in their frustration with the economic situation or political status quo. Conservatives across Germany were already up in

Hitler marched in at the head of 600 Nazi stormtroopers

arms. Bavaria was threatening to cede from the Republic, under its conservative State Commissioner Gustav Ritter von Kahr (1862–1934). He had announced a great rally in the Munich *Bürgerbräukeller* – a vast beer hall, often used for gatherings of this kind – for the evening of 8 November, to drum up enthusiasm for this move.

Adolf Hitler flanked by Alfred Rosenberg (left) and the veterinarian Friedrich Weber, co-conspirators in the Munich *putsch*.

Defiant stormtroopers await the signal to go into action before the Munich _putsch_ of November 1923.

In the event, his meeting was hijacked; his audacious plan upstaged by an even more daring one as Hitler marched in at the head of 600 stormtroopers. Not content with Bavarian secession, he and his supporters (who included Hermann Göring and Rudolf Hess) demanded nothing less than a 'national revolution'. Von Kahr, at first delighted at what seemed to be the appearance of formidable political reinforcement and military strength, was taken aback when he realized the extent of the Nazis' zeal, and quickly withdrew his support.

THE COUP COLLAPSES

Hitler called on all present to join him and his stormtroopers in a Mussolini-style March on Berlin where they would precipitate the resignation of the government and seize power. They got as far as a nearby army barracks, which they occupied along with the local police station, arming themselves for the ensuing stage of their triumphal path to power.

In the event, it was all to end ignominiously the next morning when they found themselves surrounded by a government force and broke and fled. It was not quite the heroic encounter Hitler had been promising. It might even have seemed comic had it not been for the loss o f life: four police officers had fallen in the attack on their headquarters; 16 Nazis were killed in the brief battle with the troops.

Found hiding out at the nearby home of his friend and co-conspirator Ernst Hanfstaengl, Hitler was arrested and brought to trial on a high treason charge. Duly convicted, and sentenced to five years' imprisonment for plotting the downfall of the state, he was sent to Landsberg Prison, outside Munich, to serve his term. The hunt was on for Hitler.

CHAPTER 5

MY STRUGGLE, MY SUCCESS

The Munich *putsch* had flopped into fiasco; the March on Berlin into bathos – but Hitler's enthusiasm was determinedly (perhaps dementedly) undimmed. As serious as his shortcomings were, his ability to set aside failure and press on would be central to his ultimate success.

Hitler's reaction to Germany's defeat in World War I had been wildly extravagant, but it had been rational. He had recognized his country's humiliation for what it was. It's a measure of how far he'd come along the road of personal delusion that he seems to have seen his arrest and imprisonment as a sort of heroic victory – one that was worthy of recording in a memoir with the almost comically self-glorifying title, *Mein Kampf* ('My Struggle'). When it was published in 1925 (a second

Opposite: The *Führer* feeds the fawns: the future architect of the holocaust is portrayed here as a caring, nurturing spirit, protector of a pristine German nature.

volume was to appear the following year), this ranting screed was to find few readers, but within a few years Hitler would be in power and his book a big bestseller.

ILLUSTRIOUS FOREBEARS

Thrown into prison in Constantinople by the Gothic King Theodoric in 524, Boethius had written *The Consolation of Philosophy*. Centuries later, Martin Luther had taken advantage of his confinement in the castle of Wartburg to translate the Greek New Testament into German. Napoleon Bonaparte, ending his years a prisoner on St Helena, had dictated his account of one of the modern era's greatest lives. If it was good enough for these heroes of

thought, faith and military action, it was good enough for Adolf Hitler. For him, it seems, imprisonment came as a kind of vindication; official acknowledgement of his importance, and his martyr's status.

This was the tradition into which, whether consciously or not, *Mein Kampf* was conceived to fit. 'Prison literature' is not so much a genre as an exclusive 'club' – of which Hitler was understandably delighted to have had the chance to become a member. The prison setting shows the heroic commitment of the writer-protagonist; his ascetic self-denial; his forsaking of earthly liberties, pleasures and society for the sake of his cause symbolically underscored by the flagstone floor and blank grey walls of his cell. His very situation inside underlines the threat his philosophy represents to the authorities and to their status quo: he speaks for principles they can't afford to let go free.

The reality may be quite different, of course: Hitler's five-year sentence was to end up lasting less than nine months. Landsberg

The eyes have it again in the frontispiece-portrait of *Mein Kampf*, the memoir not much more than an explanatory commentary on that compelling gaze.

was an easy-going establishment as prisons went. And, far from being an outcast, Hitler seems to have become something of a pet to indulgent guards more intrigued by his notoriety than outraged by his reported views.

So far was he from being a solitary contemplative, meanwhile, that he was able to dictate his memoirs to his faithful deputy Rudolf Hess, inside with him. No matter: prison literature came with its own clearly established cachet; Hitler's powers of self-dramatization would do the rest.

BEHOLD THE MANIFESTO

What of the book itself? As its subtitle, 'A Reckoning', suggests, this first volume is a summing up, a taking stock: the biographical content only matters for the more general conclusions to which it leads. The problem for the non-partisan reader now is not so much the questionable reliability of a narrative that is at its very best self-regarding as its clear subordination of the personal to the political. We get no sense whatsoever of Hitler as a self – nor, for that matter, are we meant to, as insistently as that

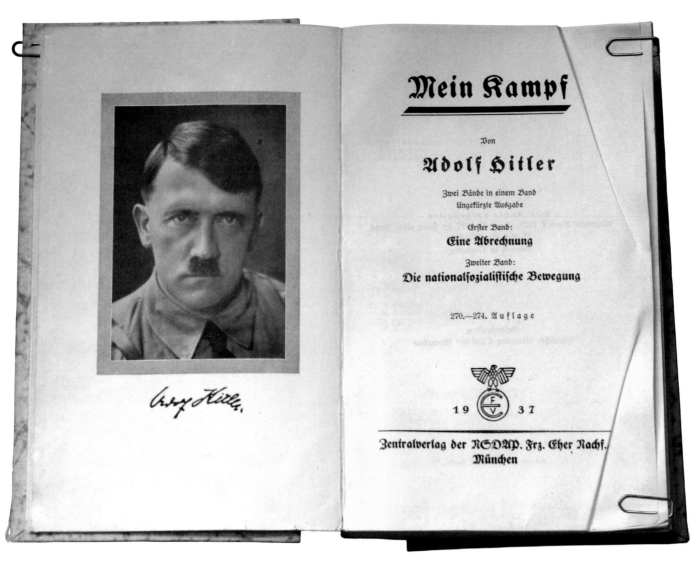

Hitler made a model prisoner – but then prison was to 'make' him as a hero for his followers, lending credibility to his political philosophy.

'I' pronoun makes its presence felt throughout.

Its autobiographical content establishes what is quite clearly a public, political persona – and a platform from which a philosophy of 'Nation' and 'Race' can be proclaimed. We are familiar with the basics: Germany, a once-proud country brought low, its pure-bred population sold out by the machinations of the Jew, in international socialism and high finance.

To begin with, sales were slow: this hardly mattered, though, for a volume whose importance was at this stage more talismanic than anything else. Handy as it might be as a propaganda primer towards which the new Nazi recruit could conveniently be steered, its chief significance was the air of legitimacy it conferred – on Hitler as its author and on his NSDAP – in an age and culture that still paid deference to the printed word. Martin Luther had brought about his Reformation through the publication of his German Bible; Hitler hoped to make modern German history through *Mein Kampf*.

MARCHING ON OR MARKING TIME?

The immediate response was underwhelming. *Mein Kampf* had given Hitler and the Nazis enough of a boost to feel that struggling on was still worthwhile, but there was no sign of their taking Germany by storm. Party membership, a minuscule 2,000 or so in 1921, had grown to 6,000 by the end of 1922 before rocketing to around 55,000 by the time of the Munich *putsch*. Since then, though, it had fallen back to less than half that number. And so the same endless round of beer-hall meetings and back-room deal making went on, with little prospect of a breakthrough any time soon.

It hardly helped that Germany's economic ills were easing as the country entered what were to be

The authorities at Landsberg could hardly have made Hitler much more comfortable. Here, he relaxes with Rudolf Hess (second left) and others.

known as the 'Golden Twenties'. As of 1924, the so-called Dawes Plan – named for America's Vice-President Charles G. Dawes (1865–1951), who had introduced it – had helped reduce the reparations burden. In the end, a movement that had originated in the chaos following World War I and the Versailles Treaty was not to find new impetus until a fresh disaster had come along.

PERSONALITY AND CULT

'Half Plebeian, half god!' Goebbels' reported remark on finishing *Mein*

Kampf in October 1925 reflects the peculiar mix of adoration and disdain one follower felt in relation to his leader Adolf Hitler. Joseph Goebbels (1897–1945) was himself seen half-derisively as the 'Little Doctor': short in stature, he had been left crippled by polio in childhood, and his humiliation had been compounded by his rejection from military service in World War I. His personal arrogance, virulent anti-Semitism, corrosive cynicism

and wild suspicion were widely felt to have been a sort of compensation for a more profound self-hatred. Another bohemian manqué, he made a more convincing intellectual than his leader. He wrote poetry and essays, and in 1926 even published a novel.

At first, attracted more by the NSDAP's 'socialist' side than by its nationalism, Goebbels had backed the party's anti-capitalist wing, which was led by Gregor Strasser

PERSONAL GREETING

Deeply disapproved of, even in those countries where it isn't explicitly illegal, the straight-arm salute is inextricably associated with Nazism now, despite the fact that Hitler and his followers had adopted it from Mussolini and his fascist followers, for whom it had been the (fittingly nativist) 'Roman' salute. There is no archaeological evidence to support this label, but it seemed the sort of thing the ancient Romans might have done.

Hitler made it his own, however – just as he was to make his party and his country his own. Made mandatory in 1926, it was known in Germany as the 'Hitler Salute', and had to be accompanied by the greeting 'Heil Hitler!' It accordingly gave the *Führer* at least a symbolic presence at every interaction – whether official or simply social – between party members, (and ultimately, by the time the totalitarian state was being built in the 1930s, at every interaction between German citizens).

Ready to break ground for the construction of the Reichsbank, workers greet their leader with a straight-armed Nazi-style salute.

(1892–1934). They believed that when workers' rights and social justice were achieved, an organic sense of nationhood would follow. While Hitler had been away in Landsberg, Strasser and his supporters had been able to pull the party in their preferred direction. In 1925, they had even got as far as attempting to organize a Leftist party coup against Hitler. They'd missed their chance, though: his authority was rapidly restored.

That Hitler and Goebbels were both able to get past this treachery to form a close political and personal relationship says much for the former's ideological flexibility and for the latter's pragmatism. Intuitively shrewd, for all his notorious volatility and rage, Hitler could when it counted overlook a personal offence in furtherance of longer-term objectives. (That he could also hold a grudge was to be clear from – among many other examples – Gregor Strasser's eventual fate, a victim of the Night of the Long Knives a decade later.) Certainly, Goebbels was to prove an enormous asset, doing more than anyone else to bring to reality his leader's vision of a National Socialist movement that would be as much about aesthetics and emotions as 'pure' politics.

Goebbels was to prove a huge asset in bringing about his leader's vision

It was Goebbels, for instance, who fashioned the story of Horst Wessel – an activist killed in a 1930 street fight – into a potent martyrdom myth; as Reich Propaganda Leader of the NSDAP, indeed, he was to become the great myth-maker to Hitler himself. 'Nation', 'Society', 'Germany', the 'Workers'... the main terms of the

Left: A wayward supporter at best, Gregor Strasser had strong views on the Party's political direction: these finally led to a fatal falling-out.

Opposite: Physically slight and short on charisma, Goebbels made up for it in personal devotion, political fervour and propagandistic genius.

Already a hero after his exploits as a fighter pilot in World War I, Hermann Goering makes a striking SA Commander, 1923.

NSDAP's title were all effectively abstractions. In the personality of the *Führer* they found both an emblem and a living force. It was in the nature of Nazism that myth, rhetoric and reality were closely and dynamically related. A rabble-rousing speech of Goebbels' was in 1938 to be the trigger for *Kristallnacht*.

HIGH FLIERS

Another friend from these early days was Hermann Goering (1893–1946), ultimately to be the *Luftwaffe*'s commander-in-chief. He was a famous flying ace himself; a hero of World War I, and in 1922 the natural choice to head the SA Brownshirts. A veteran of the

---

Goering had shed blood for the Nazi cause, having been shot in the leg

---

following year's Munich *putsch*, he even shed blood for the Nazi cause, being shot (with appropriate ignominy) in the leg. From these faintly farcical beginnings, he went on to help set up some of the most secretive and repressive institutions of the Nazi state, including the Gestapo; he was also involved

in planning and establishing the first concentration camps. Hitler's accessory in the organization of the Night of the Long Knives in 1934, he was also to be its main beneficiary, being promoted to a position of leadership within the SA. With Hitler and Goebbels he was to be another important architect of the Final Solution. After his conviction of war crimes, in 1946, he was to commit suicide in his prison cell.

Rudolf Hess (1894–1987) was to be Deputy *Führer* from 1933. He first met Hitler in 1920 and they quickly found Far Right

Rudolf Hess (centre) stands with co-conspirators outside the *Burgerbräukeller* in the hours before the ill-fated Munich *putsch*.

Surrounded by stormtroopers, Heinrich Himmler holds the banner for Nazism at the height of the Munich *putsch* of 1923.

enthusiasms in common. Hess, a student of geography after his front-line service in World War I, was to influence his friend in formulating his theories of *lebensraum*. Although afterwards famous in the West for his one-man flight to Scotland in 1941 in quest of peace (or, at least, of Aryan alliance), Hess was a willing and eager disciple of Adolf Hitler. At his side during the Munich *putsch*, he served time with Hitler in Landsberg where, as his leader's secretary, he took down his dictation of *Mein Kampf*.

Also among those present in the *Bürgerbräukeller* for the Munich *putsch* had been Heinrich Himmler (1900–45). He was eventually to wield immense and cruel power as *Reichsführer–SS* and Gestapo chief. For the moment, though, earnest and bespectacled, he seemed an anonymous, even mousy, figure.

The idea of 'administrative flair' would have seemed oxymoronic to Hitler or Goebbels – though this perhaps showed how much they needed someone who possessed this quality in their party. Himmler did most certainly. Without him, neither the NSDAP nor the Nazi state could ever have become what they eventually did. His organizational instincts came out more chillingly in the detailed ambition of his plans to perfect the Germanic master race by means of mass murder and selective breeding.

It was to be in Himmler's slipstream that Reinhard Heydrich (1904–42) would sweep to power. Comparatively late to the NSDAP cause, he got involved in the early 1930s after his dishonourable discharge from the German Navy. Quite how dishonourable he'd really been is debatable: as painful as his decision to back out of his engagement to another young woman to marry Lina Mathilde von Osten (1911–85) may have been for his originally intended, the resulting marriage was to prove enduring.

It was a marriage of two fascistic minds, and it seems to have been through Lina's wider family that Heydrich found his way into National Socialist circles. There, his soldierly swagger and stereotypically 'Aryan' good looks quickly caught Himmler's eye (as an idealized 'alter ego'?). He was to be dogged, despite this, by never proven yet persistent rumours of a Jewish ancestral 'taint'. These may in turn have helped fuel a chronic insecurity and vicious paranoia that otherwise sat oddly in one who seemed the ultimate Nazi 'Superman'.

Eastern Europe came to know Heydrich as the 'Blond Beast'. He began organizing the imprisonment and annihilation of Poland's Jews

LOVE AND LOYALTY

No one went back further with the *Führer* than Ernst Röhm (1887–1934). They met for the first time in 1919. The two young men had much in common – not least their experiences during World War I. It has been suggested that the homosexuality that, though only latent (if there at all) in Hitler's make-up, was in Röhm open and unabashed. Neither he nor his deputy Edmund Heines (1887–1934) made any secret of a sexuality they seem to have seen as an extreme expression of a soldierly comradeship. Far from being effeminate, in this view, homosexuality was hyper-masculine; far from being gentle or tender, it bonded in acts of brutal violence.

Notoriously private, even secretive, about the more inward feelings and intimate aspects of his life, Hitler made no effort to distance himself from his friend's behaviour. On the contrary, he allowed Röhm (and only Röhm, among the Nazi leadership) to address him by the informal and more intimate *du* form rather than the more official *sie*. Whether this showed where his true sexual sympathies lay, as some historians have thought, or was just the *Führer*'s refusal to be bound by the same social taboos as lesser men, we have no way of knowing.

Besides, by 1934, it didn't matter. If Hitler's continuing support for Röhm in the face of criticism had shown his long-term constancy, just as striking was his willingness to renounce that seeming loyalty when it suited him. Fearing the growing power his friend had been accumulating at the head of the SA, he made Röhm the first target of his Night of the Long Knives.

Ernst Röhm seems to have been closer to Hitler than anyone else for several years. But that very closeness would bring him down.

promote their ideology of hate. As unemployment soared (to upwards of four million by the end of 1931), so did support for the NSDAP, which by that time boasted 800,000 members. 'Boasted' is the right word, perhaps, given the suspicion that the party leadership exaggerated its strength. Even so, scholars believe there must have been 300,000 card-carrying Nazis at very least.

MARRIED TO HIS WORK?

Hitler was very much the politician now, a public figure. What was happening in his private life all this time? Hitler liked to imply, even at this early stage, that his responsibilities as leader left him no time for any sort of personal life – and there may have been some truth in this. He appears to have lived for his work, been wedded to his relentless routine of rallies and meetings; he read and wrote with furious zeal. As we've seen, the NSDAP was very much his show. He was not just its public face but its guts and brain. He didn't delegate – quite possibly couldn't, such was his ferocious paranoia; he sought to control its every member and its every move.

A character such as this might have had very little time for personal relationships; he certainly wouldn't have seen them as being central to his life. Hitler's comrades from this time recalled him striking self-consciously gallant postures in his dealings with women, flirting and offering compliments, but never admitting any to his inner councils – or, it seemed, his more private moments.

If, as has been argued, he additionally had concerns about his sexuality to contend with, or fears about his potency, it isn't hard to imagine him giving close relationships a swerve. There *is*, however, some evidence to suggest that this image of a man married to his responsibilities was exaggerated. Much speculation has centred on his relationship with his niece.

A FAMILY AFFAIR?

Geli Raubal (1908–31) was the daughter of Angela, Alois's daughter by Fanni Matzselberger. She too was an Angela – 'Geli' is a common short form – which maybe makes things seem that bit more strange. Angela Senior, having drifted apart from her half-brother for some years, went to see him in Landsberg, and they appear to have grown close again. In 1925, she started working for him as his housekeeper, with her

---

THE ONE THAT GOT AWAY?

A 16-year-old shopgirl in Alpine Obersalzberg when she first met the Nazi leader, Maria Reiter (1911–92) was destined to become a puzzling but persistent presence in his life. Even if her testimony (given many years later) is to be believed, they were only ever briefly and occasionally together as lovers. In keeping with what appears to have been a pattern among Hitler's romantic partners, Maria made an unsuccessful attempt at suicide in 1928. She hanged herself, but was found by her brother, who cut her down. Thereafter, it seems, she reconciled herself to the vicissitudes of an on-and-off relationship that was much more off than on. Their closeness survived Maria's 1936 marriage to SS officer Georg Kubisch: Hitler was seemingly to see her as late as 1938 (when, says Maria, he confided his unhappiness with Eva Braun). We have no way of confirming Reiter's claim that Hitler was several times to ask her to marry him, but his sister Paula confirmed her importance in his life.

Maria Reiter, once a shopgirl, but soon it seems the *Führer*'s lover. Little is known for certain of their story.

Hitler in relaxed pose in a deck chair next to his niece Geli Raubal, sometime around 1930.

two daughters, Geli and Elfriede. Geli would have been just 21, less than half the age of her uncle, when in 1929 she moved into his new flat in Prinzregentenplatz. In the weeks and months that followed, the two were often seen about Munich together – out for walks, or in the bars where Adolf met his cronies. They clearly got on; indeed, they were clearly close. Gossip was inevitable – even if there's no proof either way.

Hitler's psyche had surely been shaped by his emergence from a family background of borderline sinister closeness and complexity and he would have been compounding this if he'd involved himself sexually with Geli. Does that make a relationship between the two less likely? Or more likely?

It's impossible to say. Hitler's intimate emotional life appears to have been complex; the impact of his background can have been nothing if not perverse.

Whatever the nature of their relationship, it came to the most abrupt of halts when, on 19 September 1931, she was found dead, shot with Hitler's pistol. She'd been talking of leaving for Vienna, it was said – weary of her uncle's hyper-possessiveness. Had he killed her? Or (given that by all accounts he'd been away in Nuremberg at the time of Geli's death) had he given the order that she be killed? Or, perhaps most probable, had she shot herself…? Even by this

time, Hitler had gained himself so large and loquacious a collection of enemies and enthusiasts that it was impossible to see through the slander and speculation to any sort of truth. That possibility has only receded further in the historiographical hysteria of the post-war period. It remains one of surprisingly many mysteries in Hitler's life.

FOREVER EVA

Geli's replacement as Hitler's girlfriend – if that was what she was, and what Geli *had* been – Eva Braun (1912–45) enters the narrative at this point. In fact, she may have first met Hitler as

Eva Braun, in full colour, as befits the *Führer*'s mistress, holds in her lap a cutesy (but faintly risqué?) pussy-cat.

long ago as 1925 when she'd been working as an assistant to his personal photographer. While there's no suggestion of any other contact at that point, they do seem to have met again, and to have started seeing each other – at least occasionally – in 1929. At that time, she was 17 and he was 40, but he wouldn't have been the first 'strong' man to prefer his female partners young and tractable. After Geli's death, Eva may have started to be a partner of some sort: they seem to have seen each other a great deal more.

> ## On Eva's side, at least, there was a relationship, and it was intensely felt

It is impossible to know exactly the nature of their relationship – what they did in bed, or if they ever even made it there. The speculation on Hitler's possible sexual hang-ups and handicaps has been rich and highly varied, and there's no way for these doubts to be resolved.

On Eva's side, at least, there was a relationship and it was intensely felt. Hitler's commitment may have been more lukewarm – or maybe it just had to be, given his continuing determination to appear to be the leader married to his country; the strong man without a softer side. That would be the obvious inference to be drawn from a (deliberately?) bungled suicide bid of August 1932 in which Eva shot herself across the chest. Could the echo of Geli's suicide have been

coincidental? We can't know, but it seems unlikely. Eva was to make a second attempt in 1935, this time taking an overdose of sleeping pills. We've no way of knowing how determined this attempt was either, though presumably it reflected continuing frustrations with her relationship with Hitler.

Once again, we cannot ascertain where those frustrations lay – for all the entertaining theories about her lover's 'micropenis' and so forth. The reality is, regardless of

Hitler's style-choices haven't always lasted well: in its day, though, this carefully composed portrait would have communicated youthful idealism and strength.

how happy and fulfilled or not Eva was in her intimate moments with Hitler, those moments were often few and far between. Ever conscious of appearances, the *Führer* seems to have felt he had to cut her in public; she had to come and go to his quarters in the

Hitler and Goebbels chat over a 'one-pot' supper. Encouraged by the Nazis to foster social feeling, the money saved was given to the poor.

utmost secrecy. For Erich Kempka (1910–75), Hitler's chauffeur from 1934 to 1945, Eva was 'Germany's unhappiest woman'.

DIETARY REQUIREMENTS

Although there's some question over exactly when it started, there's no dispute that, at least in his latter years, Hitler became a strict – and vocal – vegetarian. Not content with serving his dinner guests meat-free food (albeit cooked to the highest standards), he'd dish up lengthy disquisitions on the virtues of his philosophy. As far as can be ascertained, his attitudes were founded in an ethical concern for animals, their lives and welfare,

and in obscure theories about the purity of the human diet. According to Goebbels, part of his plan for post-war Europe was going to be a wholesale changeover to vegetarianism for all, a measure too radical to be attempted before German victory had been achieved.

Not surprisingly, subsequent commentators have made great play with the paradox of one of history's mass murderers expressing such concern for the feelings of cattle, sheep and chickens. But while we can be scathing about what we may see as his inconsistency, we can

hardly accuse him of insincerity in his views. Testimony abounds from those who saw him physically wincing at the sight of cruelty to animals or showing tearful emotion at the thought of a pet in pain.

Where exactly he came by these views and how this sensibility became so central to his personal philosophy remains unclear. It's true that his hero Richard Wagner had been a vegetarian – and intriguing that his case offers some of the same seeming contradictions.

For the composer, the meat prohibition appears to have been

his everyday reminder to himself of the empathy or 'fellow feeling' he experienced for others. When he saw an animal maltreated, he said, he suffered with the victim. 'I see in this fellow-suffering', he continued, 'the most salient feature of my moral being, and presumably it is this that is the well-spring of my art'. As counter-intuitive as it may be for us to conceive of Wagner's corrosive genius as being based on compassion, he doesn't seem to have seen any incongruity in his stance.

A *FÜHRER'S* BEST FRIEND

Dogs were widely kept by soldiers in World War I, doing sterling service as canine couriers and early-warning gas-detectors. Terriers were especially prized for their capabilities in keeping down rats. It was in pursuit of one such rodent that one English-owned Jack Russell terrier is believed to have wandered into Hitler's trench in France. Hitler had famously befriended him and named him Fuchsi ('Little Fox').

Hitler's soft-hearted fondness for animals has intrigued historians given his cruel reputation where humans were concerned. Witnesses report the man who cheerfully went to see political enemies being tortured, executed and their bodies hung up on meat hooks being unable to watch filmed scenes of animals being hurt or killed.

Cruelty and sentimentality came together, perhaps, in his especial love of the German Shepherd breed – an affectionate pet and a wolf-like predator rolled into one. Hitler had a series of these dogs, most famously Blondi, who went with him to his bunker in his final days. Having had her killed, in the hours before his own suicide, Hitler was inconsolable.

Adolf and Eva loved their dogs, his an appropriately imperious German Shepherd, hers the more ladylike and playful Highland terrier.

out of retirement before that, to lead the Eighth Army on the Eastern Front, in World War I. By 1932, then, he was well into his eighties. It seems to have been as much under pressure from the liberal left and centre as from his own more conservative supporters that he let himself be persuaded to run for office one last time. Only a man with his unimpeachable military credentials could have convincingly stood out against the

warlike rhetoric of Hitler and his Nazis, it was felt. A career soldier, well advanced in years, he had all the makings of a crusty 'Colonel Blimp' type, but he remained a firm believer in democracy. He seems to have felt almost personally affronted by Hitler's style, so would not have needed much persuasion to stand against him.

Von Hindenburg did succeed in keeping Hitler out of the presidency when the Nazi leader ran against

Opposite: The stalwart German farmer mucks out the nation, tossing out Jewish financiers and communist agitators in a Nazi election poster of 1932.

him in the elections of March and April 1932. Despite the support of a range of democratic allies, however, he wasn't able to prevent the NSDAP from becoming the largest single party in the Reichstag – a position consolidated in further elections that July. When a renewed attempt to break the impasse failed that November, Hindenburg saw

Hitler's speaking style was widely mocked abroad, but millions of Germans found it mesmerizing: here he addresses an election meeting in 1932.

The burning of the Reichstag was to leave German democracy a gutted shell: Hitler used it to justify wielding despotic power.

uneducated labourer with learning difficulties, van der Lubbe was very likely used as a dupe by Nazi provocateurs.

The burning of the Reichstag, blamed on the communists, was the excuse Hitler needed to call for a clampdown on left-wing dissent and the cancellation of a range of fundamental freedoms. Hindenburg had no alternative, he felt, but to issue what became known as the 'Reichstag Fire Decree' allowing the rights to assembly to be suspended and powers of internment without trial to be introduced. He finally caved in and rubber-stamped an 'Enabling Act' – whose passing he had for some weeks being resisting – allowing Hitler effectively to govern by decree.

DISPENSING WITH DEMOCRACY

Although presented as emergency legislation, the Enabling Act was to remain in force for four years, so it certainly didn't feel like a 'temporary' measure. Moreover, backed up by a government that was itself protected by the terms of the Act, the NSDAP was able to extend its campaign of violence and intimidation at street level. Armed SA took up positions inside Parliament itself to keep an eye on things once the Reichstag had been reconvened in the temporary surroundings of Berlin's Kroll Opera House. The Catholic Centre Party having cautiously conceded its backing to Hitler on condition

no alternative but to appoint Hitler as Chancellor of Germany, in January 1933.

FIRE ALARM

If Hitler's elevation had already dragged the Reichstag into ignominy, things were soon going to get much worse. On 27 February, the parliament building was burned down. Arrested at the scene, a Dutch communist, Marinus van der Lubbe (1909–34), was tried and convicted of arson; he was executed for his crime the following

year. From the first, though, there had been suspicions that the Nazis themselves had set the fire that was ultimately to allow them – at least figuratively – to send the constitution up in flames.

Van der Lubbe was indeed to be defended during the post-war period as the victim of a cynically deliberate miscarriage of justice, and was finally formally pardoned in 2007. In fact, few historians share the German government's confidence in his innocence – although it's acknowledged that, an

that Hindenburg would retain a veto, Hitler had the parliamentary majority he had been seeking.

An 'elective dictatorship', it turned out, could be just as brutal and repressive as a 'real' one. On 2 May, stormtroopers smashed up trade union offices; they arrested their leaders and whisked them off to concentration camps. Next, it was the turn of the more moderate social democratic parties. Harassed and bullied, they were forced into backing down.

The next group to get it was the SA leadership, most notably Hitler's old street-fighting friend Ernst Röhm, who were purged in a

FROM ARTISTS' COLONY TO CONCENTRATION CAMP

The *Munich Illustrated Press* carries an upbeat account of the 'educational' regime at Dachau, 16 July 1933.

as a whole seem to have objected strongly.

Dachau had the dubious distinction of being the first of the Nazi concentration camps, opening its gates on 22 March 1933 – just a few weeks after the Reichstag Fire. Those held there were, for now at least, overwhelmingly left-wing activists. Later they would be joined by Jehovah's Witnesses, homosexuals, Roma, and thousands of Jews. For now, though, the Final Solution was yet to be conceived.

Till the time of Hitler, Dachau's had been a name to conjure with – especially for artists. The young Hitler might well have dreamed of setting up here, in a city not far from his adoptive Munich but associated with such celebrated painters as Carl Spitzweg (1808–85), Ludwig Dill (1845–1940), Adolf Hölzel (1853–1934), Arthur Langhammer (1854–1901) and Lovis Corinth (1858–1925). Now the name is accursed, so closely is it identified with the camp in which so many thousands were to die.

'First they came for the Socialists …', in Pastor Martin Niemöller's famous formulation. Far from making a secret of its first round of arbitrary arrests and detentions without trial, Hitler's government boasted of its ruthless efficiency. It was only right, insisted Police Chief Heinrich Himmler (1900–45), that Leftists should be taken out of circulation for the sake of 'calm' in society as a whole. Nor does society

series of summary executions in the 'Night of the Long Knives' (actually 'Nights': 30 June–2 July 1934). This might have given more satisfaction to the *Führer*'s enemies had it not been obvious that this bloodletting was only making his own position more secure. We'll never know how many lives the 'Night of the Long Knives' was finally to claim: at least 80, it's believed, but maybe several times that number.

WIELDING THE KNIFE

Despite the macho violence of its stormtroopers at street level, the SA leadership was rather different

> *A flamboyant figure, Ernst Röhm had never made much secret of his homosexuality*

in tone. A flamboyant figure, Ernst Röhm had never made much secret of his homosexuality, and nor had many of the friends he surrounded himself with in the topmost ranks of the SA. Self-consciously

sophisticated and ostentatiously louche, they became notorious for their limousine lifestyle and for the decadent banquets they loved to hold – and seemingly with the *Führer*'s blessing.

Just how close where they? Rumours of homosexuality had dogged Hitler since World War I, and what appeared to have been his bachelor lifestyle since had invited speculation. So too did the brutal liquidation of Röhm and company in the 'Night of the Long Knives'

Hitler leaves a Munich polling station after casting his vote in a 1932 election. The Nazis were soon the biggest party in the Reichstag.

purge of 1934. Had Hitler acted to pre-empt pressure from – or even blackmail by – former friends? It's by no means impossible, although he might have feared Ernst Röhm's rise to unaccountable authority in any case: by now the SA was becoming his private army.

CHRISTIAN FORGIVENESS

That summer, Hitler agreed his infamous 'Concordat' with the Vatican. Pope Pius XI was anxious to secure the rights of Catholics in Germany. More so, it seems, than to send a clear signal about what was already quite clearly an evil regime with nothing but contempt

Right: The partnership between Hitler and Röhm was to end with the latter's liquidation. For now, though, both personally and politically, they were close.

Below: The God in his own religion, Hitler held Christianity in contempt. He saw his 'Concordat' with the Vatican as a necessary compromise.

Statesman or soldier? Hitler took considerable pains to present himself as both, as in this official portrait by B. von Jacobs (1933).

Hitler had been hard at work on his cult of personality since the 1920s: *Mein Kampf*, the 'Hitler Salute', his comrades' constant toasts ….all these things were intended to boost his myth. At a certain point, however, what had been a curious eccentricity of a marginal minority had become mainstream politics; now, with his ascent to power, it was the German way. That personal, emotional dimension to supporters' adulation was just as present as it had been when Goebbels had first marvelled at his majesty on finishing *Mein Kampf*, except that now it extended across vast swathes of the German nation. Just how exalted his authority now was becomes clear when we consider a song (or, rather, 'hymn') now popular among the Hitler Youth, as reported by a crestfallen Catholic bishop of the time:

> *We are the merry Hitler Youth;*
> *We have no need of Christian*
>   *virtue,*
> *Because our* Führer *Adolf Hitler*
> *Is our redeemer and*
>   *intermediary….*

A PYRAMID OF POWER

Hitler saw himself as the apex of a pyramid of power, supported immediately by his Chancellery and private staff. Below him were a pair of deputies, with their staffs, who in turn presided over a tier of 18 Reich leaders with responsibilities for the whole range of party organizations (from the SA and SS to the German Women's Association and Hitler Youth) and affiliated bodies (including state-sanctioned professional groups and workers' 'unions'). Below came the district leadership; and subordinate to them were the county leaders to whom in turn the local chapter leaders would report. And so it went on, through the 'block leaders' – who represented (and reported on) party members and the public at street level – to the individual members in their homes.

Although this pyramid represented only the hierarchical organization of the party, it doubled as a paradigm for power in the country. As of 14 July, when the 'Law Against the Formation of New Political Parties' had been passed – or just decreed – the NSDAP was the only party allowed in Germany.

TOTAL TRANSFORMATION

'Everything within the state; nothing outside the state; nothing against the state.' Mussolini had

Hitler addresses workers at the Siemens engineering plant, Berlin, in 1933. His SS bodyguard stands just behind the dais.

in 1928 elegantly articulated the principles of what would come to be known as 'totalitarianism'. To say that Hitler sought control would woefully understate the reality. One-party rule made possible the imposition of one single vision – political, social, economic and even aesthetic. Hitler the artist could set to work on his greatest creation. By the time he was finished, no corner of everyday life, no living moment, would remain untouched. Hence the formation of a corporate state: private business was brought into a mutually supportive partnership with the Nazi government. Hence too the creation of the Hitler Youth to inculcate the values of Nazism in the young – and, indeed, of the National Socialist Women's League to ensure that these same values were sucked in with mothers' milk.

The 'socialist' strand in the NSDAP's title has been controversial. Hitler was no socialist as that term has generally been understood. No state-administered sharing economy, in other words; no wealth redistribution; no 'From each according to his ability; to each according to his needs'. But the word did reflect the readiness of the Nazi state to intervene in every aspect of the country's life, from the construction of autobahns to the funding of public health campaigns. Such interventions were by no means necessarily unenlightened: they included action against

A Nuremberg Rally from a megalomaniac's eye-view: if Hitler's speeches electrified his supporters, what must their adulation have done for him?

industrial pollution, breast cancer screening programmes and anti-smoking ads. The other side of the coin was an unprecedented intrusion of official scrutiny into what had previously been 'private' life.

State interference was by no means invariably this benign. Education became a system of indoctrination into Nazi thought on everything from family values to racial theory. 'Health' care encompassed the forced sterilization of those deemed to carry mental or physical defects for the 'protection' of the German nation as a whole. The category of 'mental' defects, moreover, included not just what we might now regard as real mental health issues, but everything from criminality to sexual licence.

'BLOOD' AND 'HONOUR'
Then, of course, there were the racial policies. Anti-Semitism, for centuries an ingrained habit, now became the official attitude of the German state. As early as 1933, Hitler had called for a national boycott of Jewish-owned shops and businesses, which had hit that community hard. Now, with the Nazis in power, its effects were harsher still. In the summer of 1935, what had been a murky mesh of suspicion, resentment and unreflecting hatred was given legislative force in the Nuremberg Laws (so-called for the scene of the party rally at which they were announced). Under a 'Law for the Protection of German Blood and German Honour', mixed marriages were outlawed – as in general were sexual relations across racial lines.

A new Reich Citizenship Law stipulated that only those known

Nuremberg wasn't just about big set-piece speeches. Here, Hitler chats with Gertrud Scholtz-Klink of the Nazis' Women's League.

to be of German blood could claim the rights of citizenship. Jews were explicitly excluded from holding these rights, which meant their ineligibility to work in the main professions or the civil service. Many middle-class Jews were plunged into poverty. Their new non-person status effectively legitimized casual harassment and abuse. If the obvious answer was emigration, that option was anticipated and to an extent forestalled. Aliens had to hand over up to 90 per cent of their savings as a 'tax' on leaving.

The popularity of such measures with the mass of Germans makes a mockery of any attempt to absolve the nation as a whole or to brand Hitler as sole author of what was to become the Holocaust. He had, however, been sole author of an actual book, *Mein Kampf*, in which the nature of the 'Jewish Problem' – and the need to 'solve' it – had been meticulously mapped out. There's no doubt that the Nuremberg Laws, sorely as they discredited Germany in general, represented the ugly triumph of Hitler's racial thought.

BEAUTY AND BLUSTER

It would be naive to imagine that the philosophy of race extended only to human biology or ethnography. Hitler could see degenerate 'racial' characteristics in the arts as well. To some extent, his hostilities seem little more than highly theorized rationalizations of suspicion that self-consciously respectable members of the middle class worldwide have always felt for the unfamiliar and new. 'Judge for Yourselves,' said the slogan at the exhibition of 'degenerate' art the party organized in Munich in 1937. This 'rogues' gallery' was to include Picasso, Matisse, Van Gogh, and many more of what we think of as the titans of twentieth-century painting: but the Man on the Heidhausen Tram was to be the arbiter of artistic value here.

The objections of the Nazis went well beyond petit-bourgeois bluster, though. Hitler couched his philistinism in his own more idiosyncratic, more sinister terms. The view of the Nazi architect Paul Schultze-Knaumburg (1869–1949) that work of true artistic merit would appeal as much to the 'healthy SA man' as to any connoisseur makes it clear how militaristic aesthetic thinking had become. The odd use of the word 'healthy' here underlines how deep

the ideas of purity, wholesomeness and (on the other hand) of degeneracy now went.

INFLAMMATORY IDEAS
These ideas underlined the wider suspicion of the totalitarian Nazi state of any artistic or intellectual community that sought to exist autonomously, without reference to official views or values. The Great Book Burning of 10 May 1933, organized by Goebbels, was as much a general assertion of authority on the part of the

new government as it was a specific attack on ideas of which it disapproved.

Many of those whose books were burned were well-known Leftists like the playwright Bertolt Brecht (1898–1956) and novelist Alfred Döblin (1878–1957); or they were Jews like Heinrich Heine (1797–1856), Franz Kafka (1883–1924), Stefan Zweig (1881–1942) and Joseph Roth (1894–1939). Or, of course, they were both, as Rosa Luxemburg (1871–1919) and Walter Benjamin (1892–1940)

Stormtroopers, lighting up the night with torches, call for Germany's streets to be swept clean of Jews (1935).

had been – along with the great ideological grandfather of them all, Karl Marx (1818–83).

Cosmopolitan in their contempt for ideas, the Nazis burned books by foreign writers from H.G. Wells (1866–1946) to André Gide (1869–1951). Books by Ernest Hemingway (1899–1961) and James Joyce (1882–1941) were consigned to the flames as well, their crimes (presumably) avowed left-wing sympathies and literary obscurity respectively. It could hardly have been a coincidence that the central figure of Joyce's genre-busting novel *Ulysses* (1922) had been one Leopold Bloom, a Dublin Jew. No more than it could have been that it was Sigmund Freud, the descendant

Cosmopolitan in their contempt for ideas, the Nazis burned numerous books by foreign writers

of generations of rabbis, who had been first to formulate and theorize the idea of the subconscious and all the unwholesome desires and instincts that seethed and surged therein. The works of Freud were burned, of course, as were those of other enemies of decency Albert Einstein (1879–1955) and Leo Tolstoy (1828–1910).

Hitler's word, the Party's doctrines; no decent German would ever want to enquire more deeply. This was the implicit message of the book burnings.

BLUE NOTES

Then there was the response to jazz, embraced as much by sophisticated musicians as by the socialite elite of Germany's great cities. A new, American import, with strange tonalities and syncopated rhythms, jazz music must genuinely have shocked its first German hearers, however broad-minded they may have been.

Hitler, however, fastened on the colour of its most famous performers – African-American, of course – and on the Jewish backgrounds of such celebrated composers as the Gershwin brothers George (1898–1937) and Ira (1896–1983) and Irving Berlin (1888–1989). 'Bastardization' was becoming the norm, Hitler had lamented in a 1928 speech; 'Negro music is dominant, but if we put a

Duke Ellington jams with friends, 1939: the improvisatory anarchy of jazz was almost as threatening to the Nazis as its racial 'taint'.

Beethoven symphony alongside a shimmy, victory is clear.'

Many educated people of the time, not just in Germany but elsewhere, would have judged the works of Beethoven to be somehow 'higher' and consequently 'better' than that of any ragtime or swing band. A great many respectable householders would have feared the culture of alcoholic excess and lax morality they associated with this music and the kind of clubs in which it was performed. And it would be idle to pretend that the presence of black performers would not have alienated the average German burgher – even if, for his would-be-rebellious sons and daughters, it may have added to their allure. Hitler took this fear and developed it into a

thoroughgoing theory of jazz as musical miscegenation.

The same prejudices seem to have held further up the artistic hierarchy. German Expressionism is now remembered as one of the glories of the artistic twentieth century. In its day, though, it too was denounced as 'negroid'. How can a picture or sculpture display the character or qualities of a human ethnicity or race? For many, though, the claim made sense – by intuitive analogy, if not by any logic.

What jazz did with its virtuoso black musicians, the new movements in the visual arts were doing with their wilful disregard for old conventions and with

an improvisatory anarchy that matched the reckless energy of jazz. As Paul Schultze-Knaumburg explained, the difficulty of such art – its extraordinary departures from established conventional norms; its tendency to abstraction and consequently to obscurity – reflected the 'Jewish longing for the wilderness', and hence for the 'Negro' and his 'Savage' world.

It's true that many modern artists – most famously, perhaps, Pablo Picasso (1888–1973) – had been drawn to the directness and emotional immediacy of so-called 'Primitive' art. Others, from surrealists like Max Ernst (1891–1976) to Expressionists like

Hitler makes his first radio broadcast to 'his' people as Reich Chancellor after gaining power on 1 February 1933.

Wassily Kandinsky (1866–1944; a Russian-born master who had made much of his career in Munich) and his disciple Paul Klee (1879–1940) went about their search for 'wildness' in ways that didn't owe anything to this more anthropological idea of 'savagery'. Still less could anything have been said to be (in any meaningful sense) 'negroid' about these works.

JEWISH – OR JUST DIFFICULT?

For the most part, the works marked out for denunciation as 'Jewish Art' were not actually by Jewish artists – those of Marc

Chagall (1887–1985) were the most obvious exception to this rule. The purge appears to have been inspired by the feeling that the art world more generally was Jewish, in the network of dealers, critics and curators who kept it going.

As we saw with Chamberlain's 'Chinese Jews', moreover, the moment race begins to be everything to a thinker it quickly ends up meaning nothing very much. Hence the 'Jewish' quality his critics came to find in the works of the German Expressionist painter and printmaker Emil Nolde (1867–1956) – despite his

having been an NSDAP member since 1920. Nolde's political views are a matter of record, as are the anti-Semitic insults he directed at Jewish artists. He was a disgraceful figure, but there's nothing obviously 'Nazi' about his creative works. He was sufficiently innovative to fail Schultze-Knaumburg's 'healthy SA man' test, however – there were no blonde-haired, apple-cheeked maidens or idealized landscapes among his works.

In fairness to men like Nolde, a great many of the twentieth century's greatest writers and artists had political views that seem deeply unfortunate in hindsight. Famous novelists such as D.H. Lawrence (1885–1930) and Joseph Conrad

(1857–1924) – both, ironically, victims of the Nazi book burnings – and internationally renowned poets such as William Butler Yeats (1865–1939) and T.S. Eliot (1888–1965) shared Hitler's impatience with what they saw as the debasement of existence under modern capitalism. They also shared, to some extent, his hankerings for a less sceptical and cynical, more mythic and organic past. They weren't to have the same opportunity Nolde would to see the effects of this kind of political philosophy at first hand, but they certainly shared some of the same prejudices.

Fierce anti-Semitism; NSDAP-membership: even these couldn't protect Nolde's art from the stigma of 'Jewishness' in the Nazis' topsy-turvy aesthetic order.

ARTISTIC DIFFERENCES

The arbitrariness of the artistic code by which the works of an anti-Semite like Emil Nolde could be denounced as 'Jewish' prompts the question of whether other factors might have influenced this violent backlash in the arts. It does appear that internal party politics came into play. Hitler, at the start of his artistic 'career', though admittedly

conservative in his own work, had not been obviously hostile to the avant garde. Nazi film and propaganda were in many ways profoundly innovative. Joseph Goebbels had harboured ambitions as a poet.

Goebbels appears to have championed some quite adventurous art – like Nolde's. But he was bitterly opposed by Alfred Rosenberg (1893–1946). A Nazi *avant la lettre*, Rosenberg had joined what was then the German Workers' Party nine months before Hitler himself had and he'd looked after the NSDAP shop while Hitler had been in Landsberg. Rosenberg out-Hitlered Hitler in the demented mysticism of his thinking on everything from race and society to modern art.

This was, he said, a 'sickness' – not just figuratively but literally. By way of illustration, he compared

Alfred Rosenberg was the winner in the internal debate over art in the Nazi Party. He championed a stifling, stultifying conservatism.

the faces and forms of the men and women in contemporary paintings with photographs of people with disfigured features or birth defects. He favoured the idealized classicism

> It is no surprise that the architect of the Nazi state should have interested himself in its more literal architecture

of nineteenth-century academic art. His own vocation apparently forgotten, the *Führer* pretty much stood aside and watched while Rosenberg and Goebbels fought it out – the former triumphing in what amounted to a turf war across the arena of German art.

BUILDING THE FUTURE

From the start, the *Führer* had taken a keen interest in every aspect of the Nazi 'look'; from the design of supporters' uniforms to the party's insignia and its presentation at mass rallies. It is no surprise, then, that the architect of the Nazi state should have interested himself in its more literal architecture.

Public buildings were naturally a focus for a style that set out quite consciously to glorify the state: massive scale and grandeur underlined the power of the people when properly led. New though it might be, the Nazi style in construction was conservative, caricaturing that of classical Greece and Rome. Both those civilizations

had arguably elevated the public and imperial over the private and individual spheres. Regular and symmetrical, they gave no hint of depth or subtlety or of hidden meaning. They were safe and easy to understand.

The Nazi aesthetic is perhaps most perfectly exemplified by the Olympic Stadium in Berlin, built to host the Games of 1936. As it turned out, the stadium was to be the scene of Hitler's humiliation by the African-American athlete Jesse Owens (1913–80), who rained on his parade of Aryan achievement with his four gold medals.

There were many other examples, though: Hitler's intention was to stamp his authority and that of the Nazi state on the face of Germany. In 1937, he commissioned the architect Albert Speer (1905–81) to make over the whole city of Berlin.

EXPANSIONIST AIMS

Hitler had designs on the architecture of Europe too. It was a humiliation not to be borne, he insisted, that German-speaking Saarland and the western Rhineland should be administered by France. The arrangement, made at the Versailles Conference, had been explicitly punitive, so Hitler's objections were neither unusual nor unreasonable.

In 1935, after years of agitation, the League of Nations authorized a plebiscite in which Saarland's inhabitants voted to be part of Germany. Emboldened by this step, Hitler had his soldiers occupy the Rhineland the following year, to test the French response. None was forthcoming – Hitler's rise had thrown the Western European governments into a paralysis of panic – and the territory was reabsorbed into the Reich.

SCREEN IDOL

Rumours of a romantic relationship were never to be proven, but there is no doubt of the depth and sincerity of Hitler's veneration of Leni Riefenstahl (1902–2003). His admiration was shared by some of the most distinguished practitioners and critics of post-war cinema, who generally regarded the German director's films as classics. Riefenstahl, for her part, fully reciprocated her *Führer*'s feelings: her movies are clearly labours of love – even if the exact constitution of that love is obscure.

Where *Triumph of the Will* (1935) records and thrillingly dramatizes the events of the Nazi Party Congress of 1934, *Olympia* (1938) makes an epic of the Berlin Games of 1936. Technically creaky as they seem now, these films vividly recapture the excitement of those toxic times. In important ways, too, they haven't aged. Bringing real creativity to crass propaganda, genuine artistic innovation to the articulation of a familiar message, Riefenstahl brought Hitler's vision to exhilarating life on the movie screen.

Cinema was the one area in which the Nazis accepted innovation, Leni Riefenstahl the nearest thing they produced to an important artist.

Although outnumbered in Europe as a whole, Hitler drew a sense of security from knowing that, with Mussolini's Italy, his country formed a stable 'axis' through the heart of Europe. What was already being referred to as the Axis was ratified by a treaty in 1936; these European powers were later joined by Japan.

Old-fashioned classicism on steroids, Nazi architecture in the shape of Berlin's Olympic Stadium inspired awe – but not much else.

These manoeuvrings along Germany's western frontier were not much more than a preliminary flexing of muscles, despite the symbolic importance of taking back territories that had been lost. In the second half of *Mein Kampf*, however, Hitler had made the case for Germany's carving out a vast area of *lebensraum* – 'living space' – in the Slavic territories to its east. 'Nature does not know political frontiers,' he had argued; rather, competition, or what he called 'the free game of energies',

gave the largest and best areas of land to the 'superior' race or species.

Such sub-Darwinian flights notwithstanding, Hitler was prepared to appeal to historical precedent and hereditary 'title' when it suited him. He reached back into ancient history for the purpose of reviving the idea of the Oium, an enormous expanse of territory along Europe's eastern edge and in the westernmost steppes of Asia taken by the Slavs from the Germanic Ostrogoths.

AT HOME WITH HITLER

As Hitler's political stock soared, so too did sales of *Mein Kampf*. What had once seemed like a loser's half-crazed scrawlings were now the compelling memoir-manifesto of the great new leader. With the money pouring in, the *Führer* set about constructing a private life appropriate to the public position he now occupied. As chancellor, he had an impressive and imposing official residence in Berlin, but he was also creating a cult of personality around himself. That meant a focus on his character and his life in its totality; its off-duty moments as important as its official functions. The idea of private life as a sort of performance

The cares of office briefly set aside, Hitler relaxes at the Berghof. Every aspect of his image was meticulously managed.

is part and parcel of today's celebrity culture, but in the 1930s it was still very new.

Hitler's instinct for image management was not to let him down. He had himself photographed looking thoughtful among leather-bound books and weighted with (stoically borne) responsibility among historical paintings in his Chancellery. But he also allowed revealing glimpses of his leisure moments in the wholesome scenery and pure fresh air of the Alps. He'd been coming

to Obersalzberg since the 1920s (this was where he'd met Maria Reiter); now, however, he was able to buy Haus Wachenfeld, the mountain chalet he had previously rented, and turn it into a fitting backdrop against which he could be seen, a man of appealingly simple pleasures, 'relaxing' in his garden in the company of his pets. From 1937, he would set about having Haus Wachenfeld rebuilt and substantially extended to become the altogether grander residence known as the Berghof.

simplicities could seem much less clear.

Hence the agreement reached on 23 August 1939, and signed by Germany's Foreign Minister Joachim von Ribbentrop and his Russian opposite number Vyacheslav Molotov. The Nazi–

> ## The 'non-aggression' pact was a signal for immediate acts of aggression by both signatories

Soviet Pact was certainly no friendship agreement; nor did it even promise mutual support. It committed both sides to staying neutral if one were attacked by a third country. Stalin's readiness to do a deal with Hitler has, understandably, been condemned by historians, especially because this 'non-aggression' pact was the signal for immediate acts of aggression

The broken glass that gave *Kristallnacht* its name was the least of it: scores of Jews were killed in this state-sponsored pogrom.

by both signatories – in Germany's case in Poland; in the USSR's in the Baltic States.

Stalin had no illusions about Hitler's attitude to him and to his Soviet state. The Western democracies would have been the lesser of two evils from his point of view. The commitment to the overthrow of capitalism was central to communism. In the early years of Russia's Revolution, the Western states had all done what they could to (in British statesman Winston Churchill's words) 'strangle the Bolshevik baby in its cradle'.

However, they did not rave about 'Judeo-Bolshevism' in the way that Hitler did. Nor did they talk of war as some kind of spiritual fulfilment or speak in reverent terms of (largely Russian) *lebensraum*. Hence the Soviet dictator made increasingly frantic overtures to the Western

BIRTHDAY BOY

The carve-up that followed the Nazi-Soviet Pact was to produce peculiar political and historical eddies – generations after mainstream history had 'moved on'. Russia's annexation of the Baltic states stirred such resentment that right-wing extremists in Estonia, Latvia and Lithuania were publicly to celebrate Hitler's birthday (20 April) throughout the

Soviet era. And beyond: in Tartu and Tallinn, Estonia, 'skinheads' have commemorated this day well into the twenty-first century; in Vilnius, Lithuania, it has been marked by attacks on Jewish cemeteries. Ironic, of course, given Hitler's role in green-lighting the 'Red' invasion in the first place – but rationalism has never been the point where Nazism, or its offshoots, have been concerned.

powers through Foreign Minister Maxim Litvinov in the 1930s, in the hope that they might join him in an anti-fascist alliance. However, when all these advances were rejected, Stalin unceremoniously dumped the (Jewish) Litvinov and the negotiations that eventually led to the 'Ribbentrop–Molotov Pact'. Ultimately, what was at stake was Soviet survival.

What was at stake for Hitler was freedom of action, in the reassuring knowledge that his Eastern front was shielded. He could wait to deal with Russia and its communists another day. In the meantime, he could look out calmly across a Western Europe in evident disarray, its leaders on the edge of panic at the prospect of another war.

FOREIGN FRIENDS

Hitler's British and American admirers were few but influential: Unity Mitford belonged to a famous (and famously colourful) aristocratic family.

US President Franklin D. Roosevelt (1882–1945) felt real alarm at Hitler's rise, but among his countrymen his concern was not too widely shared. Many Americans were of German extraction, and of those who weren't a majority were unwilling to commit to a war against a country with which they felt they had no quarrel. Hitler's anti-communism seemed commendable, if anything, while anti-Semitism was not something non-Jewish Americans could get too excited about in an age of open racism. Of America's most famous individual supporters, the industrialist Henry Ford (1863–1947) and Joseph P. Kennedy (1888–1969), US Ambassador in London and the patriarch of the Democrat dynasty, neither appears actually to have met Hitler.

Britain too was reluctant to see the danger: the loss of a generation to World War I had severely diminished any real appetite for another war. Meanwhile, many – especially among the traditional elite, who felt they had most to lose – welcomed Nazi Germany's stand against Soviet communism.

No socialist himself, but vindicated by history as more far-sighted than many of his contemporaries, Winston Churchill (1874–1965) cut a comparatively forlorn figure with his warnings against Neville Chamberlain's engagement widely unheeded. 'Country House Nazism' was a real thing: Unity Mitford (1914–48) was only the most notorious of a bevy of aristocratic English admirers of 'the greatest man of all time'. It's unclear if they were ever lovers, but she and Hitler were certainly close.

It was not only women who were smitten with the special glamour of the *Führer*: to Harold Harmsworth, 1st Viscount Rothermere (1868–1940), and proprietor of the *Daily Mail*, he was an honorary monarch: 'Adolf the Great'. But Hitler could number real kings among his courtiers, although Edward VIII (1894–1972) was to abdicate within a few months of his coronation in 1936 because of his determination to marry the American divorcée Wallis Simpson (1896–1986). As the Duke and Duchess of Windsor, the couple's continuing links with Hitler (whom they met in 1937) were to give rise to scandal and suspicion in wartime and post-war Britain.

Vyacheslav Molotov becomes the Soviet signatory to the Nazi-Soviet Pact under the avuncular eye of Joseph Stalin, 1939.

UNLUCKY 13

Johann Elser's bomb plot blew up in his face, not just missing its intended target but adding to Hitler's aura of invincibility.

On 8 November 1939, Hitler and his henchmen gathered in Munich's *Bürgerbräukeller* to commemorate the fifteenth anniversary of their first *putsch*. The celebrations ended in shock and chaos when a powerful bomb went off, leaving six Nazi officials killed and more than 60 injured.

The *Führer* had left unexpectedly early. Had the bomb detonated only 13 minutes sooner, Hitler would have been caught up in the blast. As it was, Hitler was able to incorporate the incident into his cult of invincibility. The attack had been the work (over many weeks) of trade unionist Johann Georg Elser (1903–45); he had first scouted out the hall the year before. Although trained as a joiner, Elser had for much of 1939 been working first in an armaments factory and subsequently in a stone quarry. He would take advantage of both these roles to equip himself with explosives and detonators. His homemade bomb was carefully packed into a hollowed-out place in a pillar, behind the podium from which the guests of honour were due to speak.

Elser was removed to Dachau, where he remained for the rest of the war, only to be executed on the eve of Germany's defeat in 1945.

Poland from the east just under three weeks later – in their case under the pretext of 'recovering' territory taken earlier from the Soviet Republics of Belarus, Ukraine and Lithuania. Again, apart from hand wringing, there was no meaningful response from the Western countries. Hitler couldn't help but be encouraged.

After a period of consolidation, Hitler moved on to the offensive. Eight months of 'Phoney War' ended abruptly with the invasion of France and the Low Countries on 10 May 1940. Famously, this first offensive in the west was to prove a triumph of *blitzkrieg* (literally 'lightning war'), fought at high speed, with armoured and motorized weaponry.

A British Expeditionary Force sent into France was sent scrambling for safety, isolated completely as it was by the curving arc of Operation 'Sickle Cut'. 'Nothing but a miracle can save BEF now,' wrote II Corps' Commander, General Alan Brooke. After a certain fashion, though, that miracle was worked. The Dunkirk Evacuation of 26 May–4 June – led by the Royal Navy but comprising mainly civilian ships, from fishing boats to ferries, was to save a quarter of a million French and British troops from capture. It may not have made much difference from a military point of view – the Allies had still 'lost' badly – but it allowed the beaten British to salvage some pride.

Ready for action: Hitler reviews a body of German infantry just prior to the invasion of Poland in 1939.

ANGLO-AMBIVALENCE

The British were to recover a great deal more over the weeks and months that followed, as Hitler showed his first signs of hesitation. His rhetoric with regard to Britain had always been more conciliatory than that he'd used for other countries. Had he harboured hopes that Anglo-Saxon England would rediscover its Germanic roots?

On 19 July 1940, he got as far as making a 'Last Appeal to Reason' in the Reichstag. Copies of this speech were subsequently airdropped over the southeast of England. The Nazis, Hitler almost pleaded, had never wanted anything more than to free their country from the unfair penalties laid upon it by the Versailles Treaty – and from the 'fetters of a small substratum of Jewish-capitalist and pluto-democratic profiteers'.

Historian Andrew Roberts reminds us (in his 2009 study, *The Storm of War*) that Hitler was a frank admirer of Britain's imperial achievement. Even while the fight for France was raging, he was heaping praise upon the 'civilization' Britain had brought the world. Roberts goes further, explaining what he characterizes as the 'slapdash' nature of the Nazi invasion plan as evidence that the *Führer* had no real stomach for this particular fight.

'Since Britain shows no sign of being prepared to come to an agreement despite her desperate military situation,' he'd begun his 'Directive 16', 'I have resolved to prepare – and, should it be necessary, pursue – an amphibious operation against England. The point of this operation will be to prevent the English homeland from being used as a base for the continuation of the war against Germany. If need be, the whole island might be occupied.'

> ## 'I have resolved to prepare ... an amphibious operation against England...'

There's an obliqueness about Hitler's language here, its opening clause ('Since Britain...') reading like one last plea for reason to prevail. And even when the direct threat comes, there's a certain hesitation: not 'I have prepared', or 'I have resolved to pursue', but 'I have resolved to prepare' – and only 'if necessary' to 'pursue' the invasion option. Then there's the second, justificatory paragraph, seemingly intended to appease, to reassure Britain that its occupation would be made reluctantly and in a purely defensive spirit, 'if need be'.

AN UNCERTAIN SEA LION

This might have been diplomatic tact, but there are signs that Hitler's hesitation was real: he certainly seems to have been slow to give his signal for Operation 'Sea Lion' – the invasion of England – to commence.

The plan was that an amphibious force would make its landing along a 'broad front ... from the area of Ramsgate to that of the Isle of Wight'. This far from the continent, the *Luftwaffe* would have to do duty as artillery; the German navy would provide protection on the sea itself. There was much to do, the *Führer* noted, if the invasion was to go ahead in August:

a) The English air force must be so far neutralized, both physically and in morale, that it will be able to put up no significant resistance to the German invasion.

b) Sea lanes must be cleared of mines.

c) Both entrances to the Straits of Dover, and the western approach to the Channel in a line roughly from Alderney to Portland, are to be closed off by minefields.

d) Landing zones must be covered by heavy artillery on the continental coast.

e) British naval forces should be kept occupied, both in the North Sea and (by the Italians) in the Mediterranean for the period before the invasion.

The entire English Channel, in other words, had to be tied up securely in the possession of the German navy. That meant the *Luftwaffe* had to control the airspace above it too, especially because Germany had no purpose-built landing craft to call upon: Hitler was hoping to do the whole thing using canal- and river-barges. Of the 2,000-odd craft his *Kriegsmarine* managed to commandeer in Germany and the conquered Benelux countries, only about a third were engine-powered – and their engines were designed for use in sheltered inland waterways. The remainder would have to be towed across

Opposite: With Paris in his possession, Hitler can take time out for cultural tourism with architect Albert Speer (left) and artist Arno Breker (right).

Opposite: Hitler and his generals plan strategy, September, 1939: at this stage, execution in the field was a formality.

the Channel by tugs and other powered vessels. When they reached their destination, moreover, they would have to be painstakingly and precisely moved into position so that the troops on board could be discharged in safety; the tanks, trucks, heavy equipment and materiel of every kind unloaded without loss. These were not the kind of manoeuvres that could be conducted either under heavy fire or in heavy seas. Everything was going to have to be just so.

In the end, nothing really was: the *Luftwaffe* fell down on point 'a' from Hitler's list, which made everything else either unattainable or irrelevant. Wave after wave of

German air attacks were beaten back by Britain's fighter force: by the end of September, the Sea Lion moment had plainly passed.

DIVIDED ATTENTION

'The art of leadership', Hitler had observed in *Mein Kampf*, 'consists in consolidating the attention of the people against a single adversary and taking care that nothing will divide that attention.' That strategy had served him well during his long, determined struggle for political success; he might have done well to heed it when it came to the conduct of the war. Instead, while Britain remained, in his own earlier description, 'a base for the continuation of the war', he opened a further front in the east a few months later. On 22 June 1941, Operation 'Barbarossa' got under way. Tearing up the Nazi–

Soviet Pact, Hitler had invaded Russia. With 4.5 million men, 600,000 tanks, trucks and cars and well over half a million horses, this was the greatest invasion force in history. It had to be, because it was fighting along a front almost 3,000km (1,800 miles) in length across the largest country in the world.

It also had to accomplish its object quickly and cleanly with minimum delay, before 'General Winter' came to the Soviets' rescue (as so notoriously it had against Napoleon in the nineteenth century). Hitler had allowed his armies four months to take Moscow; when they took

However formidable his invasion force, Hitler had first to get it across the Channel; to do that he'd have to defeat the British RAF.

A barn goes up in flames in the early days of the 1941 invasion of the Soviet Union. Germany's troops were soon to lose this sleek and cared-for look.

Smolensk in early August, they seemed to be on schedule to do just that. Becoming concerned that, in driving forward so fast, his armies had exposed their flanks, however, Hitler ordered a pause while thrusts were made northward towards Leningrad and south towards Kiev. He did so over the strong advice of seasoned generals like Franz Halder (1884–1972), Fedor von Bock (1880–1945) and Heinz Guderian (1888–1954), worried that important Moscow-ward momentum would be lost.

The counterattack that Hitler's hesitation allowed was not immediately successful, but it compounded the delay in the Germans' advance on Moscow and the attainment of their goal. As with the Western Allies' successful evacuation of Dunkirk, it may have been a minor setback militarily for German forces, but it gave their defeated enemy grounds for hope. Just enough hope, it seems, to stiffen their resolve for a defence to the death: while Kiev did fall, in late September, Leningrad was to sit out a legendary 872-day siege.

Opposite: It was from the 'Wolf's Lair', his heavily armoured bunker in the East Prussian woods, that Hitler directed Operation 'Barbarossa'.

Meanwhile, around Moscow, the Red Army was regrouping.

Time was on the Soviets' side: as the weeks went by and the weather worsened, German forces found themselves first mired in mud, then held back by temperatures in which engines and artillery seized up completely, while lightly clad soldiers suffered fearful frostbite. Even now, as the Soviets pushed back against them, rather than the strategic fallback the generals favoured, Hitler insisted they maintained a solid defensive line. That 'trench perspective' again? Hitler certainly showed his limitations here, not just as a tactician but as a real leader. Both Bock and Guderian were to be among the 40 high-ranking officers who paid the price for having being right by losing their positions after their army's final failure to take Moscow.

THE WOLF'S LAIR

Hitler was never self-conscious about what we might nowadays see as the naive boyishness of some of his self-dramatization. Take the nickname 'Wolf', which without embarrassment he awarded to himself. It was natural enough that, when a secret command centre for the Eastern Front came to be needed, with the launch of Operation 'Barbarossa', it should have had some of the character of a modern 'man cave', and be officially entitled 'The Wolf's Lair'. Miles from anywhere, in a wooded, rocky landscape in the remote interior of eastern Prussia, it was as wild a den as any apex predator could want. Around it, over 6 square kilometres (2.5 square miles) or so, extended an elaborately camouflaged administrative centre in which anything up to 2,000 staff were based.

The Wolf's Lair is not to be confused with the Eagle's Nest – either the little chalet created for the *Führer* on a vertiginous rock pinnacle high above the Berghof or the bunker built for him under Kransberg Castle, in the Taunus Mountains in the state of Hesse.

The Wolf's Lair proper was the centre of an extensive top-secret complex.

AL-LIABILITIES

As we saw in Chapter 5, Hitler had much sympathy with Schiller's stated view that 'the strong man is mightiest alone'. So, perhaps, might the strong nation have been. In the years before the war, however, Nazi Germany had felt a certain degree of safety in numbers. Hence the bonds that had been forged with Axis allies like Italy and Japan. Hitler's admiration for Benito Mussolini was genuine and longstanding; he had common interests (suspicion of the Soviet Union; competition with the Western Allies) with Imperial Japan. Later on, as the tide of war

1940, the Axis ascendant, and the *Führer* and *Il Duce* are all smiles. But relations with Italy would ultimately sour.

turned, he would come to see the Italians as an 'embarrassment', and even to begin with he was to find his alliances irksome in some ways. Italy's invasion of Greece in the autumn of 1940 very quickly ran into difficulties and Germany was dragged into a protracted campaign in the Balkans. It was also in solidarity with Italy that, in the spring of 1941, Hitler embarked on his war in the Western Desert of North Africa. Mussolini had been hoping to follow up his invasion of Ethiopia (1935) by occupying Egypt to create a continuous swathe of Italian Africa. The realities of desert warfare had proven more challenging than he'd expected.

More important – perhaps more unfathomable too – on 11 December 1941, Hitler insisted on honouring his commitment to the Axis by declaring war on the United States, four days after the Japanese had attacked Pearl Harbor. His decision has perplexed historians: while technically he was bound by the terms of the Axis Treaty to support Japan against its enemy, his decision to do so brought America into the European War.

HOME COMFORTS

For all the talk of *frontgemeinschaft*, there was really no comparison between the conditions being endured on the Eastern Front (where winter temperatures were dropping well below the minus 40° mark) and those the *Führer* and his high command were enjoying back in Germany. Some such gap inevitably exists – it's virtually impossible to conduct a war without one – but the discrepancy must have felt particularly stark this time. So Hitler had to lead something of a double life, downplaying any domestic comforts he was enjoying – especially the home he'd made with Eva Braun.

Theirs appears to have been a middle-class marriage in all but ceremony and name. Eva stayed at the Berghof, where Adolf joined her as often as he could. Up to a point, they were open about their relationship – she acted as hostess for the stream of important visitors who came and went each weekend – but she was never seen in public by Hitler's side. Again, the *Führer*

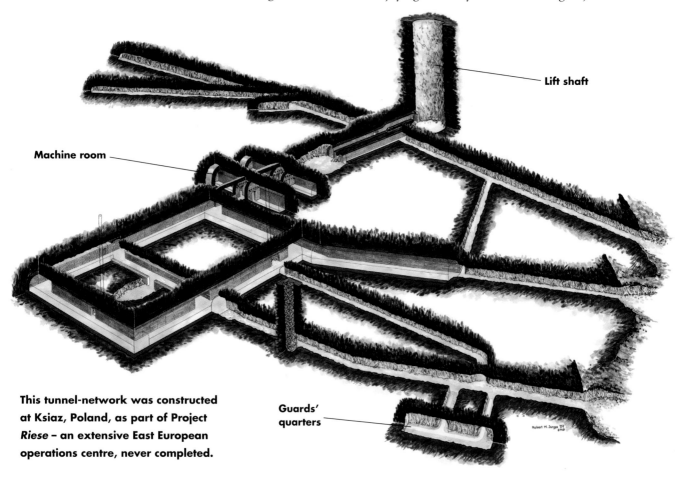

Lift shaft

Machine room

Guards' quarters

Robert M. Jurga '01
#160

This tunnel-network was constructed at Ksiaz, Poland, as part of Project *Riese* – an extensive East European operations centre, never completed.

Eva Braun enjoys the Alpine serenity of the Berghof, a world away from the war and all its travails.

Adolf and Eva look at photos in the peace and seclusion of the Berghof: images like this sent out messages of confidence and calm.

ADOLF'S ADDICTIONS

Hitler's enemies had an interest in exaggerating every oddity, but not even his closest friends disputed that Hitler had been a lifelong hypochondriac, and that his health obsessions steadily worsened towards the end. US Military Intelligence compiled a dossier listing 74 different medications he was regularly taking, while some witnesses would put the figure at nearer 90. Understandably, sensationalists have seized on the number of now-illegal drugs Hitler appears to have been addicted to, such as cocaine, heroin, and injected amphetamines (including methamphetamine, or 'crystal meth'). Potentially more disturbing, however, are the hormone-related treatments he took (in response, it seems, to some seriously unorthodox medical theories): things like testosterone, estradiol (a female hormone) and corticosteroid drugs.

This collection of medications perhaps suggests some concern about sexual performance, potency or fertility – though it's hard to see how it would have helped. They could also point to a less specifically sexual concern with maintaining energy levels in a cripplingly demanding role and a leader-like appearance of vigour and of youth. All, however, are associated with unpredictable physiological and behavioural responses, which, it's been argued, may have had some influence on his mounting instability and paranoia. Not that there's any shortage of possible causes to be found for this mental breakdown: some have blamed syphilis. But it's at least arguable that we need look

seems to have felt that he had to preserve his austere image as the warrior-leader, untouched by feminine softness of any kind. A credible logic, perhaps, although the fact that for Hitler it seemingly trumped the idea of the strong and potent woman-monopolizing alpha male surely marks him out as unusual, even among dictators. Hitler's sexuality had already been

a subject of speculation for some years, and some visitors to the Berghof were to lay significant emphasis on the fact that the 'couple' did not share a bedroom. This was hardly unusual in the period, however, and other guests – whether more soberly accurate or simply more loyal – insisted that Braun and Hitler's separate rooms had connecting doors.

Sensationalists have seized on the number of drugs Hitler appears to have been addicted to

no further than the toll being taken on Hitler by the pressures of his office and the stress of conducting a vast, complex and increasingly unwinnable war.

Such stresses might have had a bearing too on the digestive problems that plagued him (and that may have influenced his choice of a

vegetarian diet). He suffered painful stomach cramps, it seems – and, some historians have suggested, appalling flatulence. How far are such suggestions borne of an (understandable but unscholarly) eagerness to do the dictator down?

THE HOLOCAUST BEGINS

On 20 January 1942, leading Nazis came together for a special meeting in Wannsee House, a handsome suburban villa outside Berlin. The 'Wannsee Conference' is now widely regarded as marking the

beginning of the Holocaust. Not that Jews and other minorities had not been persecuted prior to this: violence, abuse and even murder had been vital to the Nazi way. It was already almost a decade since the first of the concentration camps had opened; seven years since anti-Semitism had been made official with the introduction of the Nuremberg Laws.

Till now, however, the party's war on the 'inferior races' had been pursued only haphazardly. Jews had been rounded up and executed

At the Berghof, every inch the bourgeois couple: Eva decorative and eagerly attentive; Adolf snoozing after a long hard, day.

en masse in western Russia in the course of Operation 'Barbarossa', but so had so-called 'partisans' (civilians, predominantly unarmed) in their tens of thousands. Called on Hitler's behalf by head of Reich Security Reinhard Heydrich, the Conference codified the 'Final Solution' to the 'Jewish Problem' and set in place procedures to see that it was carried out in a systematic and coordinated way.

Anti-Semitism had sounded an insistent note in the Nazi mood-music ever since the NSDAP's

foundation in the aftermath of World War I. Today, even those who know nothing else of Hitler are at least aware of his historic crimes during the Holocaust. It can come as a surprise, therefore, to realize just how late on in the Nazi narrative this racist rancour actually hardened into a stated policy of systematic murder. Through the 1930s, thinking in the party had run more along the lines of establishing a separate territory for the Jews to live in – either internally to the Reich (in a 'General Government'

Opposite: Auschwitz – ultimately, perhaps, to be Hitler's most notorious memorial – was for now a tomb into which Jews and other outcasts were daily flung.

around Warsaw) or in an offshore colony like Madagascar. As recently as 1940, members of the High Command like Himmler had been discussing the deportation of Europe's Jews – and ruing the 'cruel' nature of such a measure.

The extent of Hitler's personal culpability for the crimes committed

MORELL CODE

Hitler had his own official personal physician, Karl Brandt (1904–48): he was later to be hanged for the cruel medical experiments he'd had conducted in the camps. Monstrous as he was, though, he was a pillar of scientific rationalism and rigour beside the man who was to usurp his place in Hitler's hypochondriac confidence. Theodor Morell (1890–1948) came to the *Führer* at the prompting of Eva Braun's old boss, his official photographer Heinrich Hoffmann, rather than by any medical recommendation. On examining Hitler for the first time in 1936, he'd told Hitler that the stomach cramps he was suffering were the result of 'complete exhaustion of the digestive system'.

Hitler with Theodor Morell, the medical adviser he thought had 'saved his life', as wildly unorthodox as many of his prescriptions were.

His prescription included hormones, vitamins, phosphorus and dextrose in extravagant doses. Despite Brandt's warnings, Hitler was convinced that Morell had saved his life.

As time went on, and the *Führer* failed to improve, Morell felt the

need constantly to up his doses of the strange medications he extracted from animal intestines, testes and other organs. Not content with being a quack in his diagnoses, he cashed in on his Hitler connection, building a business empire founded on his patent cures.

Opposite: Hitler with his private secretary Martin Bormann (left), one of the least-known, yet most powerful, figures of the Third Reich.

in his name has been hotly debated ever since, and not just by those with an ideological interest in diminishing his blame. Some don't want to see the German people relieved of their responsibilities as (in Daniel Goldhagen's famous phrase) his 'willing executioners'; quite clearly, the *Führer* didn't do it on his own. There are, moreover, real questions of how authority was distributed and how orders were communicated along what could be a distinctly ragged and haphazard chain of command. Hitler's elegant 'pyramid' state-structure was in reality a much more ramshackle affair, in which section heads and regional and local officials could all enjoy a degree of autonomy.

Paradoxically, this effect was only underscored by the *Führer*'s pre-eminence at the pyramid's tip: his tyrannical caprices; his mercurial moods; his interfering interventions all helped disrupt the smooth running of the Nazi state and left lowlier officials with more to do – and more decision-making scope. None of this makes the man at the top innocent of the main charge against him. There's no serious disputing that the Holocaust was Hitler's work.

DEATH OR GLORY

Cutting a swathe through civilian populations was one thing; fighting large, well-equipped Allied forces on two fronts was quite another. On the battlefield, things were beginning to get worse. In North Africa, where till recently the swashbuckling Erwin Rommel (1891–1944) had been carrying

all before him, the Allies had regrouped and cut off a now massively outnumbered Panzer Army from reinforcements and supplies. Defeated at El Alamein (23 October–11 November 1942), Rommel gave the order to retreat, pre-empting the order he knew would come from Hitler to stand firm. That way, he reasoned, he and his men would live to fight another day.

> *For Hitler, the nobility of war transcended reason*

This was not the kind of logic Hitler seems to have understood, but for him the nobility of war transcended reason. The death-before-dishonour heroism for which he stood (or, at least, for which he expected his generals and their armies to stand) harked back to a lost age of legendary warfare. In so far as it had any relevance to modern combat, it might be argued, it was to the fields of Flanders in World War I. There, perhaps, battles had indeed been won by simply standing firm. Again, the triumph of the 'trench perspective'.

All dash and daring, high-speed advances and assaults with overwhelming force: Rommel's style of fighting till now had been the essence of *blitzkrieg*. Hitler, however, seemed more comfortable with a more cautious and static approach to fighting – just as he had when he'd held up the advance on Moscow the year before. If there

A SINISTER SHADOW

Hitler was no figurehead, but some around him still wielded enormous power: no one more than Martin Bormann (1900–45). Despite his comparative youth (he'd only joined the NSDAP in 1927), he made himself an indispensable presence in the *Führer*'s office. The head of the *Parteikanzlei* ('Party Chancellery') from 1941, he was appointed Hitler's private secretary from 1943. Rudolf Hess's flight to Britain had created a vacancy in this key position. This meteoric rise shocked sometime superiors, although arguably their

condescension had facilitated the ascent of a cunning operator too easily dismissed (like Russia's Stalin) as a brutish thug. Bormann became immensely influential – a zealous protector of the *Führer*'s interests (and his own).

If Bormann had appeared out of nowhere, he vanished much the same way at war's end. It is believed that he was shot by a Soviet patrol while fleeing Berlin. However, this was never proven; although his death was officially certified in 1973, rumours persisted of his living in exile.

was a contradiction between the forward-looking philosophy of *blitzkrieg* he believed he espoused and the more traditionalist way he'd been schooled himself as an infantryman, there was a tension too between his sense of warfare as an art and as a mere test of courage. 'How can someone be so cowardly?' he was to ask when he heard of Field-Marshal Paulus's surrender at Stalingrad on 1 February 1943. 'So many people have to die. Then such a man goes and at the last moment stains the heroism of so many others.' Was this war really being fought to secure Germany much-needed land and resources or simply as an opportunity for its men – in some strange, chivalric sense – to prove themselves?

The 'Desert Fox', Erwin Rommel, 'darling of even the enemies' news agencies', in Goebbels' words, won a string of victories in North Africa.

Stalingrad, historians agree, had been a turning point in the conflict. Hitler was to be on the back foot from that point on. The 'battle' itself had been as big as some wars, going on for five months and more, and as bloody – it's believed to have cost more than a million lives. But it is memorable chiefly for the ferocious bitterness of the fighting – from house to house and hand to hand. Paulus's Sixth Army had gone into Russia equipped for *blitzkrieg* but ended up having to inch their way towards Stalingrad (now Volgograd) through fierce resistance and over impossible terrain. Having reached the city, they'd been encircled by the Russians and, out of fuel and low on ammunition, unable to break out. They'd been forced to 'dig in', in trenches and improvised fortifications, World War I-style.

The only rational response to such a situation was surrender, Paulus pointed out. There was no pretence of rationality in Hitler's furious refusal. In the end, the commander on the ground did what he only too plainly had to do, but his *Führer* no longer dealt in realities, it seemed.

SEASICK

The *Kriegsmarine*, meanwhile, was all adrift. The well-publicized ravages of the U-boat 'Wolfpacks' in the Atlantic may have done much for morale at home (and created real consternation among the Western Allies): when all was said and done, though, this was guerrilla warfare. It hadn't been meant to be this way. In 1935, Hitler's negotiators had agreed an Anglo-German Naval Treaty, allowing Germany to rebuild its navy, so long as in total tonnage it did not come to more than 35 per cent of that of Britain's Royal Navy. The principle of rearmament once accepted, Hitler had set about taking the treaty's inch and making it a mile: the 'Plan Z' he came up with in 1937 envisaged the biggest programme of naval shipbuilding since the *Dreadnought* crisis (see Chapter 3).

The new German navy would have far more than 35 per cent of the tonnage of the British fleet. Hitler's shopping list included:
• four aircraft carriers, two of them displacing 33,500 tons

'JEWISH SCIENCE'

However high-flown his racial rhetoric, Hitler was a simple soul where science was concerned, standing for a physics of firm 'laws'; a no-nonsense Newtonianism. Modern physics, with its openness to ideas of 'relativity', its softening of what had seemed solid facts, its blurring of what had appeared to be clear-cut lines, was a transgression of boundaries. It was clearly no coincidence that these new theories should have been introduced by Jews – most famously Albert Einstein (1879–1955); nor could there be any question of their intent to attack what the Nazis called 'Nordic Science'.

Hitler had felt no qualms about hounding 'non-Aryans' out of their academic posts in German universities and colleges in the 1930s; nor even now did he regret their departure for other countries – especially the United States. 'If the dismissal of Jewish scientists means the annihilation of German science, then we shall have to do without science for a few years.' And so, to a considerable extent, they did, missing out most obviously on the atom bomb – but surely on other important advances too.

The ethics apart, what strikes us now is the obstinate inflexibility of Hitler; his unwillingness to entertain ideas or insights that differed from those he had already formed. In the intellectual arena, as in the field of war, he prided himself on being forward-looking, but flatly refused to bend to new realities.

- six battleships, of anything up to 110,000 tons
- three battle cruisers (approximately 35,000 tons)
- twelve smaller 'P-class' cruisers and two other heavy cruisers
- six light cruisers (approximately 10,000 tons)
- six large destroyers
- some 250 U-boats.

Cannily enough, Hitler had decided to go for number rather than for size of ships: the Royal Navy would still be much bigger, both in overall and average tonnage. Britain's warships were provenly potent: Germany's were going to have to run the gauntlet every time they stuck their bows outside the Baltic Sea. It made sense not to have too many maritime eggs in too few baskets – hence the decision to have more, if smaller, ships. As the smaller navy, too, the *Kriegsmarine* was inevitably going to be cast in the raider's role: speed and manoeuvrability would be more crucial than weight or power.

This was an ambitious scheme, but it was soon to peter out. Plan Z was, on the one hand, slow in getting started and, on the other, rapidly overtaken by events. Germany didn't have the industrial capacity to build so many ships in so short a time. Then there was the problem of Hitler's attention span – a difficulty his advisers would encounter daily, but that was perhaps supremely illustrated by his having started a war two years after the inauguration of a 10-year naval plan. (Not one of the ships commissioned in 1935 was ready when hostilities started.)

It couldn't help that Hitler had little understanding of or sympathy with the Navy. One warship was much like another, as far as he was concerned, and his designers' often brilliant innovations were not immediately exciting enough to hold his interest. Goering's *Luftwaffe* was consistently favouritized (in so far as the *Führer* could be consistent in anything); the capable but quietly spoken naval chief Grand Admiral Erich Raeder did not have the skill in handling Hitler that his air force rival did.

CHOPPY CONDITIONS

By the time the war broke out for real, the Germans did have three pre-Plan Z 'pocket battleships' (heavy cruisers): the *Admiral Graf Spee*, the *Admiral Scheer* and the *Deutschland*. They also had two further cruisers, the *Gneisenau* and the *Scharnhorst*. Of the Plan Z package, two battleships – the *Bismarck* and *Tirpitz* – were approaching completion by 1939; the former was commissioned in 1940; the latter in 1941. Also well under way was the aircraft carrier the *Graf Zeppelin* – but, although launched in 1938, it was never to be completed.

The loss of the *Graf Spee* off Montevideo in 1939 loomed

Its U-boat fleet was to give
Germany a rare success story at
sea: a neglected Navy struggled
to make much impact.

Hitler inspects a German warship, 1935. Planned expansion of the Navy was pre-empted by the outbreak of war.

disproportionately large, then; as did early losses off the coast of Norway. The *Kriegsmarine* found itself badly depleted at a very early stage of the war. The comparative success of Germany's U-boats – thanks in part to the genius of Admiral Karl Dönitz (1891–1980), and in part to tactical shortcomings on the part of the Allies, who were slow in organizing a workable convoy system – prompted Hitler to tear up Plan Z completely. The order went out for those ships that were on their way to being completed to be scrapped and for Germany's shipyards to go all out to build up the country's U-boat fleet. In some ways obviously a smart move, this was at the same time a defeatist one, confining the *Kriegsmarine* to a relatively marginal, harrying role.

A TURNING TIDE

Back on solid ground, meanwhile, things were beginning to look grim for Germany. A bid to take back the initiative in Russia foundered in defeat in the great tank battle at Kursk, southwest of Moscow (July–August 1943). Just a few weeks later, on 3 September, Stalin finally got something like the 'Second Front' he'd been clamouring for when the Western Allies made their first landing in southern Italy. The pressure on the Soviet Union, so long unbearable, was beginning to ease, and its armies starting to surge forward. The Germans, by no means beaten yet, exacted dreadful casualties, but they were in retreat and the Russians were pressing on.

The following summer saw the 'Second Front' opened up with a vengeance when, on D-Day (6 June), Allied forces made their landings on the Normandy beaches and began the fight for France. Just over a fortnight later in the east came Soviet Russia's Belarus offensive – Operation 'Bagration': Germany's forces were under fierce attack from either side. As for its civilians, they had for some time been under relentless attack from above, the Allies raining explosive and incendiary bombs on big industrial cities like Hamburg (the first great 'firestorm' had been recorded there, in July 1943) and smaller civilian centres like Kassel (10,000 people were killed in a single night there, in October 1943) and Darmstadt (two-thirds of whose population was rendered homeless by a single raid in September 1944). And, whenever the opportunity presented itself, they bombed Berlin.

With the odds against them stacked so frighteningly now, any German commander-in-chief would have struggled for ideas.

US troops go ashore on Omaha Beach in Normandy, D-Day, 6 June 1944. German defeat seemed just about inevitable now.

Hitler seemed bereft – his worn-out rhetoric of fighting for every inch apart. When he did attempt a bold throw – in that December's Ardennes Offensive (or 'Battle of the Bulge') – it was a warmed-over recipe from World War I. In any

A war-winning weapon – had it only been available a few months earlier: Germany's V2 heralded a new age of military technology.

case, it failed, and the New Year got under way with the Allied forces finally scenting victory. The Soviets were advancing quickly from the east as German resistance crumbled. The old East Prussian capital Königsberg (Kaliningrad) fell after a four-day siege. By February, it lay deep in Soviet territory. The Eastern Front extended 900km (560 miles) all the way from the Baltic coast to the Carpathian Mountains

of Romania. Six million Soviet troops faced around two million Germans along with some 190,000 Axis allies. In the vital central sector along the Rivers Vistula and Oder, however, the Germans were still more comprehensively outnumbered and outgunned: 11 to 1 in terms of infantry, their generals estimated; 7 to 1 in tanks; 20 to 1 in heavy artillery.

THE ELEVENTH HOUR

In the west, the picture presented to German generals was hardly more cheering. Here too a formidable force was massing. Having thrown back the *Wehrmacht* in the Ardennes, Eisenhower's army was pushing steadily towards the Rhine. With 1.5 million American, 400,000 British and 100,000 Free French soldiers, its advance could hardly be dismissed as a sideshow, but it distracted the Germans from their life-and-death survival struggle in the East. The Nazis knew that they had opened up a race war in the Slavic countries and that they could expect no mercy from the Russian troops.

Nor did they get any – although it was their country's civilian population that paid the price. Exhilarated at last to be on the enemy's own soil, the Soviet troops embarked on a spree of massacre and rape that ended only when their party commissars decided that army discipline was under threat.

The war was by no means over, though. If Germany's defeat seemed a certainty, it was still some way off being achieved. The more so because the Germans knew that nothing good could come of their conquest by the Russians: Hitler's

A COUNTERPRODUCTIVE COUP

That defeat was staring Germany in the face must have been evident to everybody but Hitler. Senior army officers weren't in any doubt. Claus von Stauffenberg (1907–44) had always remained at one remove from the Nazi true believers. Not that he was in any way a liberal – still less a Leftist. But, born into the aristocracy (he was now a count), he'd viewed Hitler and his cronies with disdain. As the hopelessness of Hitler's cause had become clear, he'd become involved with the so-called 'German Resistance' – a group of army officers, hoping to overthrow the Nazis in a coup.

Having given their conspiracy the fittingly Wagnerian codename Operation 'Valkyrie', they planned to seize power in the chaos following one of the increasingly ferocious Allied bombing raids.

Central to the success of their plan would be the assassination of Hitler: this would be done by planting a bomb in the Wolf's Lair. In the event, fearing discovery, the conspirators felt they could not wait indefinitely for the right moment. They made hasty arrangements to make their attack on the night of 20 July 1944, when Hitler would be there for a conference

Stauffenberg's bomb made an impressive mess but failed to destroy its human target.

with his officers. Stauffenberg was interrupted while he was making his final preparations and had to leave out some of the explosives he had hoped to use, making his briefcase-bomb less powerful than he had planned. Finally, when the device was detonated, the table it was hidden under helped shield Hitler from the blast. He survived – but almost 5,000 officers, rounded up in reprisal in the days after the discovery of Valkryie, did not.

German prisoners are marshalled by their Allied captors in the Ruhr. At this late stage, few felt like following their *Führer* to death or glory.

BRAIN STORM

In these final few months of the war, the writing was clearly on the wall for Nazi Germany. Naturally, Hitler rejected so depressing a reality. Only heroism would help the homeland now: epic struggle on a mythic scale – the stuff of dream and legend. What else could explain the faith the *Führer* placed in the potential of the *Volkssturm* ('People's Storm') militia that he had founded in September 1944? All males aged between 16 and 60 had to join – and bring their own clothes, rucksack, blanket and cooking utensils. In other circumstances, perhaps, an inspiring vision, but ordinary Germans had seen through their leader's promises by now; braced for defeat, they dismissed his last-stand rhetoric with sullen cynicism. They still had to serve, though – rounded up at gunpoint by the Gestapo – and so the *Volkssturm* took to the field. Never properly equipped, armed or trained, it still saw action against some of the most seasoned, battle-hardened Allied troops. Over 175,000 of its soldiers were killed in all. The call-up continued, ever more frantic as the weeks went on, gathering up younger boys – and eventually even girls.

now-customary demands for a defence to the death made sense. The East Prussian Offensive alone claimed 584,000 Soviet casualties, and over 300,000 fell in operations further south – Germany was determined to go down fighting.

It was only too clearly going down now. February had seen the Western Allies crossing Germany's western frontier and racing towards the Rhine – too quickly for effective resistance to be mounted. Many German troops had been withdrawn to the Eastern Front; those who remained were concentrated in the Ruhr. An encircling movement was soon under way to trap them there. While Montgomery's British army spearheaded the attack from the north, crossing the Rhine around Rees and Wesel in Operation 'Plunder', the American Twelfth Army under Omar Bradley (1893–1981) crossed the river at Remagen to the south. By 3 April, an entire army had effectively been trapped in the 'Ruhr Pocket' – a fatal blow to Germany's plans for self-defence.

A FINAL THROW

The nearest to a rational hope remaining was one of the various wonder-weapons then in development by teams of engineers at top-secret labs and forced-labour factories. After the set-back at Kursk, there had no longer seemed much point in taking the Panzer VIII, a 200-tonne tank. But if the moment for the *Maus* (as it was humorously called) had passed, it was hard to see the Messerschmitt

casualties – and, on top of that, disproportionate disruption, thanks to the panic and confusion they caused. Had they been ready earlier, who knows what might have happened? Had the jet come into service earlier … had Hitler had the atom bomb … Might everything have ended differently?

Heroes of the Hitler Youth are congratulated by their commander, March 1945: though surely brave, their service was a mark of German desperation.

Me262 being ready in time. This, the first battle-worthy jet fighter/ fighter-bomber, really might make a difference if the war went on long enough.

In the meantime, for the first time in a few years, the Germans were sowing consternation in southeastern England with the V1 (from *Vergeltungswaffe*: 'retaliatory weapon'), known as the 'doodlebug' from the buzzing sound it made. A flying bomb, it was essentially an early version of the cruise missile. Then there was the V2, a rocket that soared high into space before falling noiselessly down at four times the speed of sound to create completely unexpected havoc where it fell.

Both the V1 and V2 saw service in the war; both caused fearful

Where the ashes of Hitler and Eva Braun were discovered

These are impossible questions to answer – as is the one over whether Hitler's interest in these projects was more a help than a hindrance to their designers. It has been said so, by scholars who have pointed to his mercurial enthusiasms, his fleeting attention span (though both these criticisms could have been made of Winston Churchill, too). Anti-Semitism cost Hitler the atom bomb – that does appear to be true; that he hampered the development of the jet engine is more difficult to argue. Such big and complex projects invariably proceed slowly.

THE END

As the spring of 1945 approached and even Hitler could no longer doubt his country's final fate, the extraordinary scale of his delusions became apparent. Germany had proved unworthy of its destiny – and of him – he reasoned, so

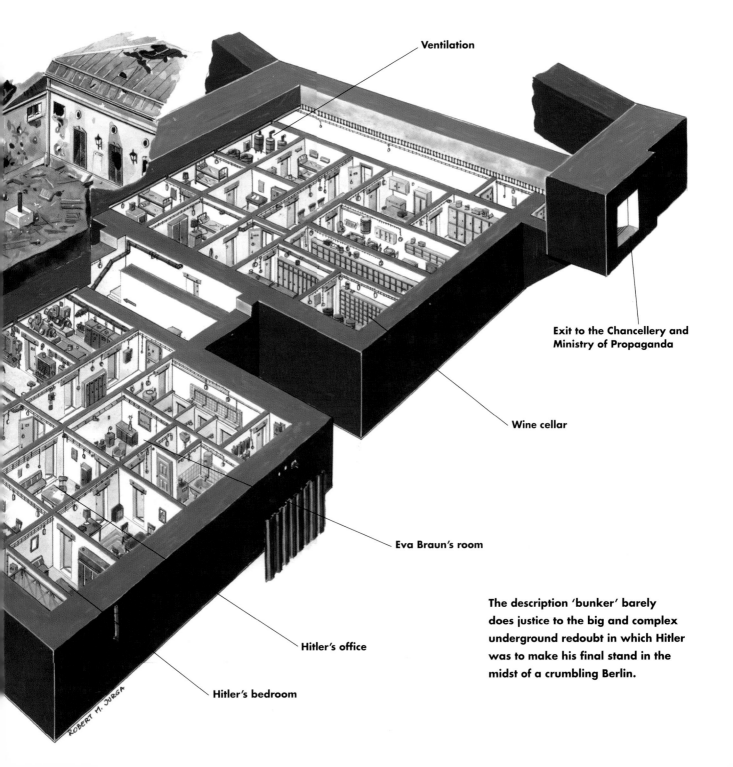

Ventilation

Exit to the Chancellery and Ministry of Propaganda

Wine cellar

Eva Braun's room

Hitler's office

Hitler's bedroom

ROBERT M. JURGA

The description 'bunker' barely does justice to the big and complex underground redoubt in which Hitler was to make his final stand in the midst of a crumbling Berlin.

some great act of national self-immolation was required. Rather than remain to go into production for some Russian or Western invader, he insisted, the country's industrial infrastructure should

Burned and scattered papers cover an abandoned desk inside the *Führerbunker* in Berlin. After the war the bunker was levelled by the Soviets.

be deliberately destroyed. There should be no Germany for any conqueror to occupy. Charged with the task of seeing this through, Albert Speer instead schemed with leading industrialists to sidestep the order.

On 29 April, with the Russians already in the suburbs of Berlin, Hitler and his staff holed up in his *Führerbunker*. He had resolved to take his own life rather than

fall into enemy hands. He is said to have been troubled by the unceremonious stringing up of Mussolini by Italian Partisans that same day, but it's hard to imagine him being able to bear being captured in any case. He had tried to arrange Eva's escape, but she insisted on joining him in his bunker to die at his side. Her romantic gesture was rewarded: the couple was married there and then.

Red Army troops give war correspondents the tour, showing them the grave behind the Bunker in which the remains of Hitler had been found.

Paranoid to the last, Hitler is thought to have feared that the supposed cyanide capsules he'd been given by his SS contacts might be fake, so he tried one out on Blondi, his beloved German shepherd. When she died instantly, he was reassured – but also distraught, more moved by an animal's death, it seems, than by any human's.

It certainly seems to have been in complete calm that, hearing that the first Soviet troops were now approaching his bunker, he handed Eva her cyanide capsule and watched her bite it before shooting himself in the head.

Loyal staff members carried their bodies out into an open space behind the bunker, poured petrol over them and set them alight: even in death, they were not to be taken by the enemy.

He had tried to arrange Eva's escape, but she insisted on joining him in his bunker to die at his side

CHAPTER 8

A DIFFICULT LEGACY

Hitler's terrible Twilight of the Gods was to bring down darkness over Germany – and to cast a long and evil shadow across the post-war world. For most an ugly warning, to a fanatical minority he'd remain a rallying-point; an example of what extremism might achieve.

Germany had yet to surrender. State radio claimed that Hitler had died fighting for his country, a day after he'd actually shot himself. The need was to keep the soldiers fighting – it was feared that they would feel demoralized and lay down their weapons if they knew he'd deserted the cause he'd told them they should be prepared to die for.

A new narrative was under construction, moreover: surviving Nazis hoped to persuade the leaders of the West that they should forget the little matters of totalitarianism, *lebensraum* and

Opposite: Flanked by fellow officers, German commander *Generaloberst* Alfred Jodl (centre) signs the German Instrument of Surrender, Reims, France, 7 May 1945.

the death camps: their party had been about the defeat of Bolshevism and the defence of freedom. They had understood that, World War II still not quite over, the Cold War was already under way, the Western Allies looking forward to the conflict that was to come. So Hitler's story ends, as it began, in the rewriting of history. And to some extent it has continued that way since.

Hitler's appointed successor as head of state, Admiral Karl Dönitz (1891–1980), did his best with former comrades (plus a few non-Nazi conservatives) to cobble together a coalition government that would meet the approval of the West. Hitler hadn't been the only deluded one. The idea that so many offences against international law, so many inhumanities on such a scale might simply be overlooked,

was unthinkably naïve. Even so, while the worst of the war criminals were to come to justice at the Nuremberg Trials, too many had taken part for anything but a tiny handful to be made examples of.

GETTING OUT

Some Nazis, with special skills in everything from rocket science to espionage, ended up working with the Americans or the Soviets, their past passed over. Again, the Cold War had started; priorities were changing. Others, despairing of such deals, used networks of secret contacts established under Nazism to make their way to safety. Several – like Adolf Eichmann (1906–62) – seem to have ended up in Latin America, where repressive regimes were ready to turn a blind eye to what they'd been before. We have no way of knowing how many

Dönitz's 'hint' might well be right – but since when had Hitler cared about 'sense'? German surrender was still wishful thinking on the London *Evening Standard*'s part.

made their way to safety along these 'ratlines'.

Some suspected that Hitler himself had escaped; that he was working quietly as a clerk in Buenos Aires or managing a hacienda out on the Pampas. The fire had done its work well: the remains

behind the bunker could have been anyone's. The Soviets tracked down his dentist and from their records he was able to identify some scant jawbone remains as having belonged to Adolf Hitler and Eva Braun. But who could be sure that he was telling the truth? Or that the

Russians were? Historiographical gossip abhors the kind of vacuum the burning of their bodies had left behind.

The German body politic was soon unrecognizable as well. The country was dismembered, split between a Communist East (the so-called German Democratic Republic, DDR) and a capitalist West; Berlin, a little exclave in the East, was itself divided. Even so, there were continuities: officially, a policy of 'de-Nazification' was pursued; in practice, the party's totalitarian hold had been so complete that just about anyone with responsibility in public or business life had been a member or had made some sort of accommodation with the authorities. Few could claim to be completely uncompromised.

AN EVIL EMBLEM

The old Reich Chancellery, in Soviet-administered East Berlin, was quickly bulldozed by the Communist authorities. They wanted the memory of Hitler and his Reich to be erased. Emblematically, however (hard as it is to imagine that this could have been intentional), they left the *Führerbunker* beneath it undisturbed. Not until the end of the 1980s was this hideout demolished. Till then, like its former occupant, it endured as a presence underground. Hitler's memory had become taboo, which also meant that it had become a source of fascination; a subject into which thousands felt they had to delve. Not just because they shared his views on the Jewish or the Bolshevik 'Problems' – although

Neo-Nazis were certainly starting to exist (while some had never gone away) – but because, like all 'forbidden' knowledge, it exercised a strong imaginative sway.

> ## *Not until the end of the 1980s was the* Führerbunker *demolished*

Freud, who had died in 1939 having fled the Nazi menace just the year before, would readily have understood this continuing appeal. In history, just as it had in life, Hitler's symbolic presence seemed far to transcend his actual significance – as important as that was. He wasn't just a dictator; wasn't just a mass murderer, even. The equivalence some conservative scholars sought to draw between him and Stalin didn't quite ring true, as monstrously evil as the Soviet dictator had been. In the memory of Hitler, however, the twentieth century's recognition that it had an ungovernably violent *id*, a destructive deathwish, appeared to have found a universal icon.

Our unruly, selfish, animalistic subconscious can either be psychoanalyzed or suppressed; honestly acknowledged and addressed or swept under the conscious carpet. Decent people, democrats tried hard to understand how Hitler had been able to come

to power in a modern democracy and how he'd gained the consent of a civilized people for (or, indeed, their enthusiastic assistance in) his crimes. Others chose denial; decided to explain away his influence (rather as he would have done himself) as a reaction to the national humiliation inflicted by defeat in World War I and the austerity imposed by a vindictive Versailles Conference. And, of course, the resulting rise in left-wing politics in Germany.

Few would go the extra mile and endorse the *Führer*'s denunciation of the Jews. Indeed, explicit supporters generally play down or deny this aspect of his legacy. 'Holocaust Denial' has been made a criminal offence in many countries (including Germany). Elaborate explanations have been offered to prove that the Holocaust was a hoax and never happened; that it *may* indeed have happened but that Hitler didn't know; or that

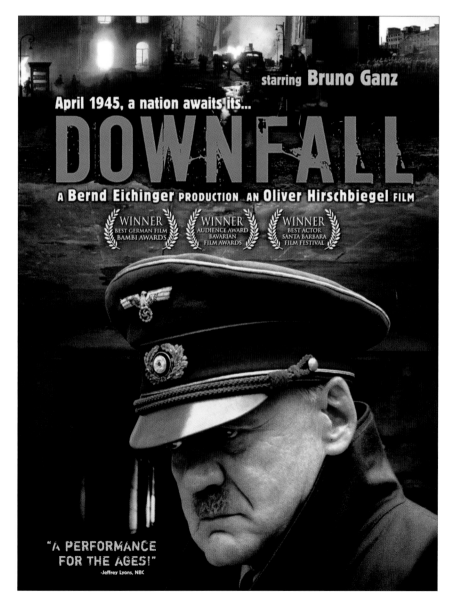

April 1945, a nation awaits its...

DOWNFALL

starring **Bruno Ganz**

A **Bernd Eichinger** PRODUCTION AN **Oliver Hirschbiegel** FILM

WINNER BEST GERMAN FILM BAMBI AWARDS

WINNER AUDIENCE AWARD BAVARIAN FILM AWARDS

WINNER BEST ACTOR SANTA BARBARA FILM FESTIVAL

"A PERFORMANCE FOR THE AGES!"
-Jeffrey Lyons, NBC

The acclaimed 2004 movie *Downfall* dramatically depicts the final days of the Nazi regime and Hitler's suicide in the *Führerbunker* with Eva Braun.

something happened but on a far smaller scale than we've been told.

A MORAL MEASURE

If denial is a danger, so too is the historiographical hyperbole that would have us see Adolf Hitler as unique. As strange as it is to think of someone so obviously and utterly guilty of his crimes as in any way a scapegoat, the view that he represents some sort of absolute of evil may offer a perilous precedent. The injunction always to remember the Holocaust as the ultimate inhumanity, without precedent or parallel, may result in its effectively being removed from history altogether. How is it to serve as a warning to subsequent generations if other genocides – in Rwanda or South Sudan, for example – can never quite measure up? The uniqueness of the Holocaust in its scale and deliberation is difficult to dispute, but is this really a difference in moral kind, or just in degree?

Conversely, when Western politicians want to liken every dictatorial Tom, Dick or Harry to Hitler, we can come to feel our ethical currency is being debased. Finding an appropriate measure is a real challenge. Hillary Clinton may have much work to do before she justifies the Hitler comparisons she has sometimes drawn, but are such comparisons never justified? The Iraqi dictator Saddam Hussein (1937–2006) had dissidents tortured and killed; pulled a gun at a cabinet meeting and shot an official who disagreed with him; he deployed chemical weapons

Seated front row, left–right, Goering, Hess, Ribbentrop and Keitel hear their destinies decided at the Nuremberg Trials (November 1945 to October 1946).

Soviet soldiers patrol what's left of Berlin in the days after defeat. The whole of Germany was, quite literally, in ruins.

against his own people and started a war with Iran that cost a million lives or more: is a comparison of him with Hitler allowable or not? Cynics pointed out that, before their falling out with him, Western governments had praised Saddam for the stability he had brought to a volatile region: did that vitiate the Hitler comparison when they came to make it?

CONCLUSIONS AND QUESTIONS

No biography can enable us to answer such questions as these definitively, especially one so brief and sketchy as this one. And challenging and contradictory as his character was, Hitler hardly seems unique in any one respect. If we can come to any conclusion, it's that he was shaped, and his evil formed, by a concatenation of different circumstances: familial, social, political, historical and cultural. If we seek to account for him and for his crimes by any one of these factors, we have no hope of finding an adequate explanation. Millions of sons in history have been beaten and seen their mothers abused without becoming mass murderers; many have endured harsher poverty or led lives of thwarted ambition – many thousands of them in early twentieth-century Vienna alone.

That said, the damage done to Hitler in childhood could hardly be clearer and must have been immense, as we have seen, while that strange temperamental

Opposite: For some, the imagery of 1929 would exert an emotional and political 'pull' long afterwards. Hitler remains a far-right icon to this day.

Saddam Hussein addresses Iraqis prior to his overthrow by coalition forces in 2003. Tyrannies come and go, but Hitler's remains their yardstick.

blend of dreaminess and rage he grew up with in hindsight seems inherently unstable. And if he was just one of innumerable Europeans weaned on race theory, his eager literal-mindedness made such ideas especially hazardous for him; just as his romantic imagination made him a risky target for the bits of bastardized Nietzsche he knew and the snapshot images he had from Klimt. A whole generation of German-speaking Austrians had, just like him, to come to terms with

sharing 'their' country and their empire with a 'porridge of nations', but most would have found other focuses for their existences, other objects of admiration and targets for resentment. Even so, when we consider Hitler's life and times, we can't help see that those two things were in crucial ways closely, even inextricably, connected. This is why, while acknowledging that a book like this can't adequately explain the man or his misdeeds, it still makes sense to find out all we can.

APPENDIX: THE REICH CHANCELLERY

The *Reichskanzlei* (Reich Chancellery) was Hitler's seat of power in Berlin. It was a vast complex, designed to overawe visitors with its grandeur. The plan of the chancellery here shows the building after its extensive reconstruction by Albert Speer, a redevelopment that cemented Speer's influence within the Third Reich. Hitler was extremely interested in every aspect of its design, as he felt it had to express National Socialist ideology – he once stated that 'Berlin must change its face to adapt to its new mission'. The chancellery was eventually demolished by Soviet occupiers after the war.

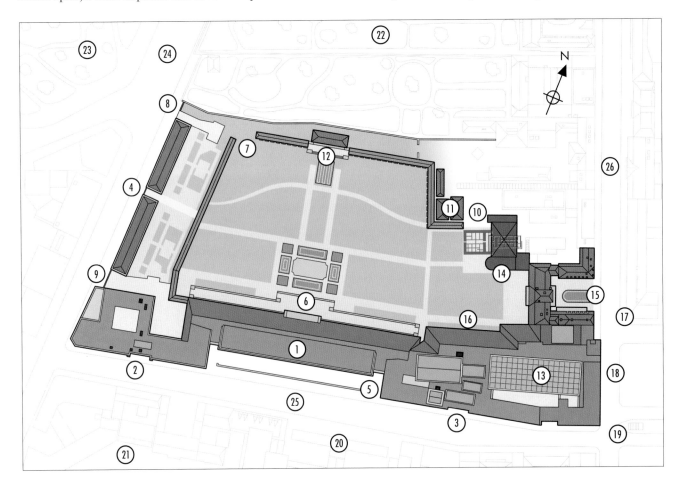

1 *Mittelbau mit Marmorgalerie* (Mittelbau Marble Gallery)
2 *Eingang zur Reichskanzlei* (Entrance to the Reich Chancellery)
3 *Eingang zur Präsidialkanzlei* (Entrance to the Office of the Reich President)
4 *Kasernenbauten* (Barracks Buildings)
5 *Hebebühne zu den Katakomben* (Lift to the Catacombs)
6 *Gartenportal zu Hitlers Arbeitszimmer* (Garden portal to Hitler's Office)
7 *Bauzufahrt zum Führerbunker* (Entrance to the Führer Bunker)
8 *Zufahrt – Tiefgarage und Führerbunker* (Access: Underground Parking and Führer Bunker)
9 *Einfahrt – Tiefgarage und Feuerwehr* (Entrance – Parking and Fire Brigade)
10 *Zufahrt – Führerbunker* (Access – Führer Bunker)
11 *Haus Kempka* (Kempka House)

12 *Gewächshaus* (Greenhouse)
13 *Ehrenhof* (Courtyard of Honour)
14 *Festsaal mit Wintergarten* (Ballroom and Conservatory)
15 *Alte Reichskanzlei* (Old Reich Chancellery)
16 *Speisesaal* (Dining Hall)
17 *Propagandaministerium* (Ministry of Propaganda)
18 *Erweiterungsbau zur Reichskanzlei* (Reich Chancellery Extension)
19 *U-Bahn-Eingang Wilhelmsplatz* (Wilhelmsplatz Subway Entrance)
20 *Kaufhaus Wertheim* (Wertheim Department Store)
21 *Leipziger Platz* (Leipziger Plaza)
22 *Ministergärten* (Ministry Garden)
23 *Tiergarten* (Animal Garden – Zoo)
24 *Hermann-Göring-Straße* (Herman Göring Street)
25 *Voßstraße* (Voss Street)
26 *Wilhelmstraße* (Wilhelm Street)

BIBLIOGRAPHY

Browning, Christopher R. *The Origins of the Final Solution: The Evolution of Nazi Jewish Policy, September 1936–March 1942* (London: Heinemann, 2004).

Dwork, Debórah and Van Peit, Robert Jan. *Holocaust: A History* (London: John Murray, 2003).

Evans, Richard J. *The Coming of the Third Reich* (London: Allen Lane, 2003).

_____. *The Third Reich in Power, 1933–1939* (London: Penguin, 2005).

_____. *The Third Reich at War: How the Nazis Led Germany from Conquest to Disaster* (London: Penguin, 2008).

Gilbert, Martin. *Kristallnacht: Prelude to Destruction* (London: HarperCollins, 2006).

Johnson, Eric and Reuband, Karl-Heinz. *What We Knew: Terror, Mass Murder and Everyday Life in Nazi Germany* (London: John Murray, 2005).

Kershaw, Ian. *Hitler 1889–1936: Hubris* (London: Allen Lane, 1998).

_____. *Hitler 1937–1945: Nemesis* (London: Allen Lane, 2000).

Merridale, Catherine. *Ivan's War: Inside the Red Army, 1939–1945* (London: Faber, 2005).

Overy, Richard. *Russia's War* (London: Allen Lane, 1998).

Roberts, Andrew. *The Storm of War: A New History of the Second World War* (London: Allen Lane, 2009).

Roseman, Mark. *The Villa, The Lake, The Meeting: Wannsee and the Final Solution* (London: Penguin, 2002).

Stern, J.P. *Hitler: The Führer and the People* (London: Fontana, 1975).

_____. *The Heart of Europe: Essays on Literature and Ideology* (Oxford: Blackwell, 1992).

Wasserstein, Bernard. *On the Eve: The Jews of Europe Before the Second World War* (London: Profile, 2012).

Willett, John. *The Weimar Years: A Culture Cut Short* (London: Thames & Hudson, 1984).

Wistrich, Robert. *Who's Who in Nazi Germany* (London: Routledge, 1995).

_____. *Between Redemption and Perdition: Essays on Modern Anti-Semitism and Jewish Identity* (London: Routledge, 1990).

Wolf, Hubert and Kronenberg, Kenneth. *Pope and Devil* (Cambridge, MA: Belknap, 2010).

INDEX